— Christmas
2005 —

Open to God,
Open to the World

D1642629

To —

Dear Marjorie & Ray
with all good wishes
& much love,

Angela

Open to God, Open to the World

CARDINAL FRANZ KÖNIG

Edited by
Christa Pongratz-Lippitt

BURNS & OATES
A Continuum imprint
LONDON • NEW YORK

Burns & Oates
A Continuum imprint
The Tower Building, 11 York Road, London SE1 7NX
15 East 26th Street, New York NY 10010

www.continuumbooks.com

First published 2005

British Library Cataloguing-in-Publication Data
A catalogue record for this book is available from the
British Library.

ISBN 0–8601–2394–4

Typeset by Kenneth Burnley, Wirral, Cheshire
Printed and bound by Cromwell Press, Wiltshire

I dedicate this book to *The Tablet* –
which has given me such joy
for over 70 years

Contents

Acknowledgements

I am especially indebted to my colleagues at *The Tablet* for their patient efforts to update my English after 40 years of living abroad. A big thank you also to Mary Stewart, one of my oldest friends, for going out to Strawberry Hill for me, where *The Tablet* archives are housed at the moment, and copying out extracts from wartime issues for me by hand. As she is not fond of modern technology and does not even have television, I was very moved when she even invested in a fax machine for my sake so that she could check parts of the manuscript for me. I would also like to thank Malcolm Walker of the Keston Institute for letting me have an article by Cardinal König on his visit to China. And last but not least, a big thank you to Dr Annemarie Fenzl, Cardinal König's right hand for so many years, for her help and co-operation.

Christa Pongratz-Lippitt

Introduction:
Cardinal König and 'his' *Tablet*

I first heard of Franz König in 1956. I was working at the
War Office in London when a friend from Austria rang
to say he had 'great news'. Franz König – 'a simply wonderful man' – had been appointed Archbishop of Vienna.
Three years later I married an Austrian and moved to
Austria permanently. In 1962 on a visit to Rome we stayed
with an aunt, whose husband was the Dutch ambassador
to the Vatican at the time. The Council was of course the
talk of the town. Our hosts gave several dinners while
we were there and on one such occasion I sat next to a
German monsignor, whose name I have long since forgotten, but who spent the entire evening talking to me
about Cardinal König and how lucky we were in Austria
to have such a brilliant and wonderful Cardinal. König
spoke several languages fluently and had even taught
himself Russian, he said. That roused my curiosity. I had
read Russian at Oxford and was most impressed that
anyone could teach themselves to talk it fluently. (The
Cardinal later enlightened me. Although he had bought
himself a Russian grammar soon after leaving school, he
did not get very far, but later found an excellent native
speaker to teach him in France.) From then on I began

to keep an eye open for anything the Cardinal wrote or
said on the radio, and my earliest newspaper cuttings,
which have long since turned yellow and are very brittle,
go back to the late 1960s. I was particularly interested
in his trips to Eastern Europe during the Cold War.

I did not get to know the Cardinal personally until I
became the Vienna correspondent of *The Tablet* in the
late 1980s. After one of my first press conferences the
Cardinal came up to me and said in English, 'So *Tablet*
[he never used the definite article] now has a correspondent in Vienna. How wonderful! Will you be staying
long?' On hearing that I lived here permanently and
had been asked by *The Tablet* to report 'occasionally'
should there be any news 'of world importance' to report,
the Cardinal said that Vienna was 'a fairly quiet place'
as far as Church news was concerned, but asked if he
might ring me occasionally to chat about *The Tablet* and
brush up his English. From then on he rang regularly. He
told me that, with the exception of the war years, he had
been reading *The Tablet* since his student days in Rome
in the late 1920s and had known Douglas Woodruff, editor
of the publication from 1936 to 1967, quite well. When
Father Jacob Gapp, an Austrian priest who refused to say
'Heil Hitler!' and was executed by the Nazis in World War
II, was beatified in 1996, and the Cardinal learnt that one
of the reason's for Gapp's execution was because he had
distributed *The Tablet* in Spain, he asked me to photo-
stat a few copies of the paper from the war years when
I was next in London. He studied them with great interest and even found a detailed report about a Slovenian
priest he knew who had been warned in time and had fled

Introduction

to Italy before the Gestapo could arrest him. The Gestapo man who warned him reminded him that Hitler was determined not only to exterminate all Jews but also all Catholic priests, and the very fact that he existed and said Mass was considered anti-Nazi propaganda. If he did not flee he would be sent to a concentration camp where priests and monks were treated 'like dogs'. 'What I wouldn't have given to read my *Tablet* in those years!', König said quietly. 'It was only on very rare occasions that we got any reports at all of what was really going on and then only when one or other of us was able to listen to the BBC . . . a terrible time, indeed!'

König loved England, the English language and the English way of life. 'Coming as I did from a small village in Lower Austria, where everyone was Catholic and spoke only German, I remember how impressed I was on my first visit in the early 1930s by that aura of the big wide world. I was suddenly surrounded by people who were more familiar with India, Australia, Canada and South Africa than with Europe, and most of whom were not Catholic.' What impressed him most, he always said, was English people's tolerance. But what interested him most was, of course, the situation of the Catholic Church in England which was so very different from the situation of the Church in Austria. Converts from Anglicanism fascinated him. He was a great admirer of John Henry Newman and visited Littlemore several times. 'I literally sometimes felt Newman's presence at Vatican II,' he once said.

I soon got used to always having my *Tablet* close at hand in case the Cardinal rang, as he would often inundate me with questions. 'Have you read the article on page 702? Quite fascinating! Who is the author? Is he a cradle Catholic or a convert? Do you think you could find out for me, and perhaps ask Mr Wilkins for his address?' A lively correspondence between the Cardinal and the author would often follow. Once, when I knew we would need St John's Gospel for an interview on inter-religious dialogue, I took my Pocket Canon edition along. 'What is that?' the Cardinal asked immediately. I told him about the Pocket Canons and how each one has an introduction by a different well-known contemporary writer, some of whom were non-believers. He beamed as he held the slim little volume in his hands. 'What a wonderful idea!' he said, 'I can always tuck one in my pocket' and immediately ordered the whole set. I was not spared the usual questions, however. 'Who edited the Pocket Canons? How did he hit on such a brilliant idea? Was he a believer?' etc. And after studying the catalogue of the 'Seeing Salvation' exhibition, he insisted on writing to the then Director of the National Gallery, Neil MacGregor, who organized the exhibition.

It was not always easy to act as a go-between between the Cardinal and the editor. I remember once when we were in the middle of a particularly difficult and delicate passage the editor said to me on the phone, 'Couldn't you get the Cardinal to bite the bullet?' It was late at night by the time I got hold of the Cardinal, who was miles from Vienna at a hotel up in the mountains. 'Bite the bullet?' he said, 'I've never heard that one before, but I can imagine what the editor means. It sounds a little warlike for a peace-loving Cardinal, but let's see what we can do.' He did bite the bullet, albeit gently, and we made the deadline, but it was almost midnight by the time we were through.

König was a voracious reader and would often read two books on the same subject simultaneously. He studied *The Tablet*'s book reviews with special interest and often asked me to order books for him. When the review of Jacques Dupuis' book *Toward a Christian Theology of Religious Pluralism* appeared in *The Tablet* in January 1998, the Cardinal rang immediately and asked me to get it for him as soon as possible as he couldn't wait to read it. As soon as he had read it, he rang to say that he had found it quite fascinating and considered it a major contribution to present-day inter-religious dialogue. Only a few months later, in November of the same year, the Vatican Congregation for Doctrine of the Faith opened an investigation into some of the views expressed by Dupuis in the book. König again immediately rang to say he would like to defend Fr Dupuis in *The Tablet*. The Cardinal was calm by nature and rarely showed his feelings, but it was quite clear that he was deeply upset, especially when he heard that Fr Dupuis had broken down and been taken to hospital. We spent the next few days preparing 'In defence of Fr Dupuis' which appeared in *The Tablet* on 16 January 1999. At the beginning of March I got an early-morning call from the editor to say he had received an English translation of a letter to Cardinal König from the Prefect of the Congregation for the Doctrine of the Faith, Cardinal Joseph Ratzinger, with an invitation to publish it in *The Tablet*. Would I please ring König, who would meanwhile also have received Cardinal Ratzinger's letter, and ask him if he would like to reply to the Ratzinger letter so that both could be published in the next issue of *The Tablet*. When I explained the situation to the Cardinal on the telephone a little later, he paused for a moment and then said in a far quieter tone than usual, 'It is a lovely spring day, the first we have had this year. I am going for a long walk and would advise you to do the same. Please tell Mr Wilkins that I will think about it and ask him to ring me back after sundown.' That evening he dictated a brief reply over the telephone in German and, after going through the English translation with me, I e-mailed it to London. Both letters were published in *The Tablet* and caused quite a stir. Two Cardinals begging to differ in *The Tablet* was certainly not an everyday occurrence.

In July 2003 Jacques Dupuis came to Vienna especially to thank the Cardinal, whom he had never met in person, for defending him. The Cardinal asked me to join them for lunch, after which they spent three hours discussing the future of inter-religious dialogue and Dupuis' latest book, *Christianity and the Religions*, over coffee. Dupuis was still very hurt about the investigation of his book. He was obviously deeply grateful for the Cardinal's support and seemed to keep seeking König's reassurance. That was certainly one of the most difficult recordings I have ever made. We were in the middle of a heatwave with the temperature nearing 40°C. As Dupuis did not speak German they conversed in English, but it was not their native language, so they often lapsed into Italian or French, or the Cardinal would explain some particularly difficult passage to me in German and ask me to translate. The three-hour recording is fine, however, and, now that neither of them is with us any longer, may one day be of historic interest.

As readers from all over the world began to respond to the Cardinal's articles in *The Tablet*, I once found the following message from him on my answering phone, '*Tablet* is making me into a "*Tablet* star", but I'm not a star. Why do you never mention my many faults?'

When Cardinal Hume got the OBE in 1999, König was thrilled. 'What an honour for the Cardinal and for the Church!' he said on the telephone, and asked me to help him word a telegram. After dictating what he wanted to say for what seeemed almost half an hour, I couldn't help remarking that this might cost quite a lot of money. 'Oh dear,' König said, 'I hadn't thought of that, but surely Cardinal Hume is worth it?' Of course he was, I assured him, but we agreed that I would ask the operator what it would cost and I would ring him back. The operator didn't speak a word of English, so I patiently dictated each word letter by letter. After a while even she said, 'This is going to cost the Cardinal a pretty penny! And it won't get there until Tuesday anyway, as they don't do telegrams any longer in England.' It was then Saturday. The Cardinal was indignant. Tuesday would not do, the telegram must get there that day. I said the only alternative was to send a fax. 'Wonderful,' he said; 'Do that!' I had to remind him that there was one hitch, however: he would have to sign the fax, so I would have to come round. There was a pause and then he said, 'I am somewhat disappointed in you. You have plenty of my signatures. Practise signing "Franz Cardinal König" on a bit of paper and don't forget to make it wobbly. I can assure you that Cardinal Hume will not mind a bit!' A few weeks later Cardinal Hume died. König was very sad. 'We had a great deal in common,' he said.

That autumn König agreed to be the guest speaker at *The Tablet* Open Day. We flew to London in early September. Dr Annemarie Fenzl, the head of the Vienna archdiocesan archives, who accompanied the Cardinal on all his trips in the last years of his life, came with us. We left on the first plane, which meant getting up at some unearthly hour. When I asked the Cardinal why we were leaving quite so early, he said he already had several breakfast appointments in London and a full programme for the next four days. We nearly lost him at Vienna airport as he had a habit of wandering off to chat with people he knew. He had already had breakfast before we set out, but heartily enjoyed breakfast on the plane and even asked for a second helping of scrambled eggs. 'Breakfast like a king, have friends in to lunch and never eat anything after 4.30 p.m.' was a motto he stuck to until his very last years.

One of the Cardinal's first visits was to Westminster Cathedral. After spending a long time praying at Cardinal Hume's grave in St Augustine's Chapel, he said Mass in the Crypt. As we were standing on the cathedral steps in the warm September sun afterwards, he took a deep breath and said, 'I wonder why I have always felt that the air in this country is freer than elsewhere?'

At a lunch which the Austrian embassy gave for him on our first day in London, König recalled how, on his first visit to England as a young curate in the 1930s, he decided to go to an Anglican service one Sunday. He was amazed how like a Catholic Mass it was. After the service he therefore went along to the sacristy, introduced himself to the vicar and asked where the differences lay. The vicar thought for a moment and then said, smiling, 'There is a difference. We have one collection, but you have two!'

The next day we drove to the ITV studios for an interview for *The Sunday Review*. I had been told that the Cardinal would be interviewed on why so many people were leaving the Church, which was the subject of his Open Day address. Dr Fenzl and I were watching the interview live next door when the interviewer suddenly asked the Cardinal a totally unexpected question. The government was very worried about the increasing number of teenage pregnancies in England, she explained, and the Archbishop of Canterbury had only recently said that 'the use of the morning-after pill could be part of a solution to help stop young pregnancies'. Was this not sending a very muddled message to young Christians? We need not have worried. The Cardinal did not bat an eyelid and said he thought it excellent and most interesting that the English government and the Churches were discussing moral issues, which was unfortunately not yet the case in Austria.

As we were driving back to the hotel from the studios, the Cardinal suddenly announced a change of plans. Instead of an early lunch followed by a siesta, as planned, he would ring a friend he particularly wanted to see and we would go out for lunch. It was midday when we got back to the hotel. Before he went up to his room to have a brush-up, the Cardinal turned to me and said, 'I'd like to have lunch at a small Italian restaurant somewhere round the corner so that we can walk there on foot. It doesn't have to be anything elegant – but not too full and it would be nice if the proprietor was Italian, then we could chat. Let's say in about twenty minutes.' And left me standing in the foyer mumbling, 'round the corner, fairly empty, Italian proprietor, in twenty minutes'. I walked over to the receptionist in a daze and hardly dared tell her my problem. But we were lucky. There was a small Italian bistro round the corner and the proprietor was Italian. He welcomed the Cardinal with open arms in Italian and the Cardinal was delighted.

That evening, after the Cardinal had held his Open Day address at Church House, the editor lost his way as he was leading us to the room where the reception was. We stumbled through the cellars, an adventure which the Cardinal enjoyed immensely and often referred to later, and finally landed in the Synod Hall. 'So this is where the decision was made to ordain women,' the Cardinal said looking round in wonderment. 'I am treading on historic ground.'

I had been trying to persuade the Cardinal to publish some of his work in English for a long time, but for years he just shook his head whenever I asked him. I was finally able to persuade him that it really wasn't quite fair of him only to publish in the German-speaking world. In summer 2003 he asked me to see if I could find an English publisher. When I rang him from London to say that I thought I had found one, he was thrilled. He fell that August and had to have a hip replacement but made a remarkable recovery. By November he was once again putting in a full day's work. He leant rather more heavily on his staff on his way down the aisle. 'Who would have thought that a bishop's staff would prove so much handier than crutches,' he said on one of his first outings. I interviewed him for the last time three weeks before he died. After that we just chatted whenever he asked me round or I read to him from *The Living Spirit*, a *Tablet* column he was very fond of. He used to ask me to bring as many passages by Newman as I could find. On one of my last visits he said he had just added another question to the long list of questions he was determined to ask his Maker. It would be the first question he would ask, he said. 'Why have I been allowed to die such a privileged death when so many people suffer so much and die terrible deaths. I shall be very keen to hear the answer.' When he saw the worried look on my face, he said quickly, 'It will be quite different from anything we can imagine, all I know is that it will be wonderful. Promise to go on being critically loyal and keep *Tablet* going. The Church needs it.' The week before he died, he asked impatiently why his *Tablet* hadn't come. It arrived the next day and he was able to leaf through it. He died peacefully in his sleep three days later.

I hope I have written up my interviews as he would have wished, and have not slipped up anywhere. We had got so used to working together that he would often stop in mid-sentence and say, 'We'll go through that again when you've written it up.' Now suddenly there was no one to go through it with me. He left a big gap – not only in my life but in many others.

I think he would have liked to close this Introduction with a creed he wrote in November 2003, his last Advent, for Father George Sporschill, a Jesuit priest whom he admired greatly and who works with street children in Romania and Moldavia.

For Father George

ON THE EVE OF MY LIFE

I believe in God, our Father,
Creator of Heaven and Earth,
Many peoples who speak different languages and have
    different faiths are on their way to you,
Let all those who seek you find shelter in you!

I believe in Jesus Christ,
Who proclaimed God's Kingdom in this transient
    world.
Help all those who are trying to hear your voice,
The strong and the weak,
The old and the young.
Call them to serve you so that they can learn
to be brothers and sisters to one another.

I believe in the Holy Ghost,
Who strengthens our good thoughts.
To you I commend all those who question and seek,
But also those who know.
They are all waiting for your word.
Let them seek the truth in love.

Introduction

On the eve of my life I thank you, dear God,
For my Church which is with you on its journey
   through time.
Let your messengers protect and lead our children.
Help us, together with your angels and with the
   children,
To renew the face of the earth and make it more
   peaceful.

I put my own and all our lives into your hands.

+ Cardinal Franz König, Advent 2003

Christa Pongratz-Lippitt

1

Vatican II:
The highlight of my life

The idea of calling a Council was conceived by a man at whose election no one, least of all he himself, had the slightest inkling of the crucial significance he would have for the Church, and indeed for the whole world. John XXIII was and called himself a simple man, a peasant's son – unprogrammatic perhaps – and yet he called the signals for the Council. He triggered what was to prove a momentous watershed in the Roman Catholic Church. It was he who set in motion that sea change which transformed the Church from a static, authoritarian Church that spoke in monologues, to a dynamic, sisterly Church that promoted dialogue. Himself a man of dialogue, he re-emphasized the importance of dialogue both with the world and within the Church itself.

I saw a lot of Pope John and will never forget his straightforwardness, the cheerfulness with which he approached the arduous tasks that faced him every day and his infectious sense of humour which he always had 'on tap'. The summoning of the Second Vatican Council will always remain linked to the person of this Pope.

In January 1959, while he was still making up his mind as to whether he should call a Council or not, he seemed at times to be amazed by his own courage. It was soon after he had announced that he was summoning a Council that he confided the following to me in a private audience. 'It was during the Octave of Prayer for Christian Unity in January [1959], you know, that, in view of the hurtful separation of the Christian Churches, the idea of summoning a Council suddenly came to me. My first thought was that the devil was trying to tempt me. A Council at the present time seemed so vast and complicated an undertaking. But the idea kept returning all that week while I was praying. It became more and more compelling and emerged ever more clearly in my mind. In the end I said to myself "This cannot be the devil, it must be the Holy Ghost inspiring me."' He acted fast, and shortly afterwards, on a visit to San Paolo fuori le Mura on 25 January 1959, he announced that he was summoning a General Council.

It was a bolt out of the blue even for those of us who realized that reform was necessary. I had just been made a cardinal. Together with Cardinal Montini, who later became Paul VI, and several others, I was among the first batch of cardinals Pope John appointed. I remember thinking, 'How will a General Council ever work? Will it deal only with inner-church reform or also with problems that concern the whole of mankind? Will bishops from all over the world ever be able to reach consensus on reform?' In order to understand what was going on in our minds, it is perhaps necessary to recall a little what the Church was like before the Council.

I had always had an urge to go out into the world and get to know other countries, other religions. On a visit to England as a young curate in the 1930s, I remember being fascinated by the different Christian Churches and beliefs. Unlike in Austria, where almost everyone was Catholic, here one encountered Anglicans, Baptists, Methodists, Quakers, etc. I was staying with a Roman Catholic parish priest in southern England when I discovered that there was a convent of Anglican nuns nearby. When I told my host that I wanted to pay the nuns a visit, his immediate reaction was, 'No, no. You must be careful. That might be seen as encouraging ecumenism.' 'All right,' I thought sadly, 'but why – or rather why not?' The priest's reaction was typical. The Roman Catholic Church feared ecumenism. Later, on my pastoral visits as a bishop, I soon became aware that many Catholics found it hard to accept the denunciation of non-Catholics and longed for a change in the Church's stance on ecumenism. Many of them were married to non-Catholics or worked together with them in the same concerns. And although there was already a strong ecumenical movement outside the Roman Catholic Church, we Catholics were discouraged from taking part and were not supposed to go to ecumenical meetings or discussions on the subject. We were in a fortress, the windows and gates of which were closed. The world was out there and we were inside, and yet we were supposed to go out and take the gospel message to all nations. But although we often shook our heads, we accepted the *status quo* and all those rules and regulations. And we had absolutely no inkling of how those walls could be removed.

Soon after the Council was announced, I heard that

every Council Father could take a theological adviser, a so-called *peritus*, to the Council with him. I immediately rang Father Karl Rahner, a Jesuit whom I knew well, and asked him to accompany me to Rome. I wanted a theologian who would help me to get a better grasp of the overall connections, but also to present the faith, that is the Christian *Weltanschauung*, in such a way that it moved people today and did not pass them by. I knew that Rahner was convinced that our mission was not to keep the faith locked away behind closed doors, but to go out into the world and proclaim the gospel message. When I asked him to accompany me, however, Rahner was aghast. 'What are you thinking of?' he said. 'Rome has considerable misgivings about me and my writings already. Imagine what they would say if I turned up as a council theologian!' And with that he declined. I asked him to think about it and said I would ring again later. When I did, Rahner said, 'All right, in God's name, but you must take the responsibility! Who knows what will happen when Ottaviani sees me!' I had already got to know Cardinal Ottaviani, the head of the Holy Office (as the Congregation for the Doctrine of the Faith was still called then) under Pope Pius XII. I remember bumping into him once soon after Pius XII first allowed evening Masses. He came up to me and said, 'Have you heard the latest? We may now celebrate Mass in the evening. Don't people laugh when you announce an evening Mass?' It took me a little time to see what he meant, but it was a typical Ottaviani reaction. There is a fixed order of things which must never on any account be changed – *semper idem* [always the same] was after all his motto – and as change was inconceivable, it was also in a strange way ludicrous! I was, therefore, somewhat worried about what Ottaviani would say to my bringing Rahner. So on my next visit to Rome I informed him privately. 'Rahner,' he muttered, shaking his head. 'How will that work?' He wasn't against it, just worried. Not long after the actual Council had begun, however, I saw Ottaviani and Rahner strutting up and down St Peter's together, deeply absorbed in conversation. Ottaviani was against change, but he was far more flexible than his right hand, Fr Sebastian Tromp, an ultra-conservative Dutch Jesuit, whom I knew well as he had been one of my teachers at the Gregorian. Tromp was utterly convinced that the Church was the Mystical Body of Christ and as such the absolute apogee of theology after which there could simply be nothing new. He sometimes quite unexpectedly came to visit me in Vienna. Perhaps he thought he could 'convert' me to his way of thinking.

Rahner scanned the numerous drafts and propositions that were sent out in the preparatory phase of the Council for me and was sometimes highly critical. 'The authors of this text have quite obviously never experienced the suffering a distraught atheist or non-Christian experiences who wants to believe and thinks he cannot,' he once commented. And on another occasion he said, 'These drafts are the elaborate theses of comfortable, self-assured churchmen who are confusing self-confidence with firmness of faith. They are the theses of good and pious scholars, selfless – but simply not up to today's situation.' But there were, of course, texts that Rahner approved of.

I will never forget the opening day of the Council. As the relatively young Archbishop of Vienna, I proceeded with two-and-a-half thousand other bishops down the *Scala Regio* towards the entrance of St Peter's. As I looked around me I realized for the first time that the Church was a global Church, an impression that has remained indelibly impressed on my mind. The Pope was carried into the basilica, but then got down from his portable throne and walked down the aisle between the rows of bishops. He was not wearing the papal tiara, but an ordinary mitre like the other Council Fathers. And then came his pathbreaking address in which he bade the bishops not to listen to the 'prophets of doom', but to tackle present-day problems joyously and without fear. As I looked around me I saw that all the tension and scepticism had given way to joyous surprise.

I have often been asked which I think are the Council's most important achievements. To my mind Vatican II set in motion four really trailblazing, creative and lasting stimuli. First it established the Church's universality. At the Council Sessions, and above all during the discussions in the intervals, one could see bishops of every colour and nationality in lively debate speaking many different languages. This multitude of different nationalities, languages and cultures changed the awareness of the Council. The Church laid aside its European attire, which many of us were so familiar with, and some even identified with the Church itself, and became aware that it was a global Church. That is why Latin could no longer be the universal language of the liturgy, and the vernacular was introduced.

Vatican II: The Highlight of My Life

The second breakthrough which opened the walls was
the Council's support for ecumenism. It was Pope John
himself who courageously took up the delicate issue of
ecumenism. He had spent years in Turkey and Bulgaria
and had good contacts with the Orthodox and Old
Oriental Churches. The initial decision to invite non-
Catholic observers to the Council came from him. Soon
after Easter in 1960, he took an indicative and most significant step. He set up the Secretariat for Christian
Unity, a small but high-powered body, to handle ecumenical matters, and appointed Cardinal Bea, an eminent
scripture scholar and rector of the Biblical Institute in
Rome, its president. Bea's role at the Council cannot be
rated highly enough. The very first draft for the decree
on ecumenism already went into the highly controversial subject of inter-religious dialogue, for instance, but
this was later taken out and became a separate declaration. Bea and his secretariat took over the responsibility
for inviting and looking after the observers, who were
by no means passive, as their designation might suggest,
but played an increasingly influential role at the Council.
Most of them were non-Catholic Christians. They had
eye-contact with the cardinals as they sat directly
opposite them in St Peter's, and although they could not
speak at the sessions, they took an active part in the
numerous discussion groups and conferences that took
place during coffee breaks and after the session debates.
At the beginning there were about 40 observers but by
the end of the Council there must have been close to 100.
They immediately had a positive influence on the
ecumenical climate and their role grew as the Council

progressed. They got to know many of the Council Fathers, Council documents went through their hands and their opinion was sought and valued. They were also able to rectify misunderstandings and bring in new aspects, and their opinions found their way into several Council decrees.

This was ecumenism at work, and it was first and foremost Cardinal Bea's achievement. I myself had frequent discussions with several of the observers and we often found ourselves in agreement on fundamental matters of faith, even if the actual formulation or wording was different. Already after the first session, in 1963, Lucas Vischer, a Lutheran member of the World Council of Churches with whom I had frequent discussions, compared what was happening at the Council to the 'bursting of a dam'. And I knew Oscar Cullman, Protestant Professor of New Testament Studies at Basle and Paris, well. After the Council was over, he said, 'Looking back and considering the Council as a whole, our expectations, except in a very few cases and in so far as they were not illusions, were fulfilled and even surpassed on many points.'

Another leading Lutheran theologian who attended all the Council sessions as an official observer was Edmund Schlink. Schlink was Professor of Ecumenical Theology at Heidelberg University and a leading member of the commission on Faith and Order of the World Council of Churches. He was a keen ecumenist and very outspoken. One of his interviews for the German press in September 1963 during the second session of the Council caused quite a rumpus. In it he sharply criticized

that, in one of the documents under discussion, the
Church of God was being exclusively interpreted as the
Roman Catholic Church. This insinuated that the yearn-
ing for Christian unity was the wish to return to the
Roman Church under the Pope and sounded as though
Orthodox and Protestant Christians were to be per-
suaded to leave their Church communities and return to
Rome, he emphasized.

But Schlink greatly admired Pope John and Cardinal
Bea. When Bea died, Schlink wrote:

> The death of Cardinal Bea is a great loss, not only
> for the Catholic Church but for the whole of Chris-
> tianity. He will be mourned by all people of goodwill
> . . . this humble and fatherly man reconciled the
> Christian Churches and convinced them that the
> Catholic Church's new ecumenical orientation was
> genuine.

Such praise for a Roman Catholic cardinal from an
eminent Protestant theologian was remarkable. Schlink
also had an almost uncanny capacity for understanding
the problem of papal primacy. He wrote a delightful book
called *The Vision of the Pope* which is a fictional
account of a pope's inner struggle to carry out his office
as the head of the Christian Church in the way Christ
would have wished him to. I re-read it when I was asked
to write the preface to the second edition a few years
ago and was astounded how relevant it is to the situation we are confronted with as regards the papacy today.
Vitali Borovoi, one of the observers from the Russian

Orthodox Patriarchate, was another enthusiastic supporter of Vatican II who wrote:

Both John XXIII and Paul VI were authentically 'angelic popes' (*pastores angelici*), to use the terminology of medieval prophecy. They dedicated their lives to the great work of the renewal of the Catholic Church, for Christian unity and the affirmation of the peace and brotherhood of peoples all over the world.

The third important breakthrough, which in my eyes was of particular momentum for the future of the Church, is the Council's emphasis on the importance of the lay apostolate. Before Vatican II the Church was often perceived as a kind of two-class system, with the hierarchy on one side and the laity on the other. This was a view that in part corresponded to the social structure of society at the time, which sharply differentiated between those who ruled and those who were ruled. But that was hardly the Gospel view. Vatican II states quite clearly that the Church is one communion. All of us, that is all the baptized, are the pilgrim people of God and we all share the responsibility for the Church. It is becoming ever clearer how important co-operation between priests and lay people is, but also how important the lay apostolate in itself is for the future of the Church.

I will go into *Nostra Aetate*, the Declaration on the Relation of the Church to Non-Christian Religions, in detail in other chapters of this book, but would like yet again to emphasize how important this briefest of all the

Council's declarations was and is. The Church's relations with Judaism, Islam and the other world religions have become more important than ever in the third millennium, and, if we are to avoid the clash of civilizations that Samuel Huntingdon prophesied, everything must be done to promote inter-faith dialogue.

For many, however, both inside and outside the Church, the renewal of the liturgy was the Council's most striking reform. Misunderstandings arose because the change was too abrupt and the faithful were not prepared gently enough. Many Catholics were so deeply attached to the liturgical forms they had grown up with and had been familiar with all their lives that the fact that the liturgy was now no longer in Latin but in the vernacular, and that the priest faced the faithful, etc., was almost more than they could cope with. Elderly priests found these changes particularly difficult. I still remember the despairing look in the eyes of one very old parish priest who, when I arrived to visit his parish, came up to me before Mass and said with a catch in his voice, 'I've tried, your eminence, I really have, but I just can't, I'm afraid . . .' (I told him not to worry.) And yet there have been many such changes throughout the Church's history. The Greek–Catholic Churches, moreover, who are in full communion with Rome, have never used Latin. Besides, Vatican II did not ban Latin, it merely allowed the vernacular. As far as the liturgy is concerned, we should neither overrate the new forms nor place too little value on the old forms.

A great deal has been written about the Second Vatican Council over the last 40 years and I think I have probably read most of the better-known works on the Council. One of the aspects that has often been under-rated, however, is the role played by committed journal-ists who informed the world of what was happening at the Council. The Council Fathers would never have been able to focus the world's attention on this phenomenal event without the co-operation of the media. The Church was slow to realize the importance of the media and to recognize its true value. Already in the 1930s, the English historian of Vatican I, Abbot Cuthbert Butler, strongly rec-ommended that at future Church Councils journalists should be allowed to attend the debates so that they could report what was being discussed. Butler was convinced that the mistrust, scorn and derision Vatican I had earned was due to the lack of precise information at the time. And at the International Catholic Press Conference in 1950 Pius XII criticized the lack of communication between the Church and public opinion, calling it 'a mistake, a weakness and a malady' and saying that both the clergy and the faithful were to blame. But little changed. Until Vatican II, the general policy was to let as little as possible of what was going on in the Vatican leak to the outside world.

This time, however, all endeavours to keep the Council debates secret were soon dropped, which in itself was already a sign that the Church's attitude had changed. It rapidly became clear that any attempt to hold the debates behind closed doors would have poisoned the atmosphere and given way to rumour and specula-tion. From then on everything that happened at the Council was reported. I myself was convinced that if the

Council was to be a success, it was crucial for able and committed journalists to inform the faithful and the world of what the hierarchy was discussing. Well before the Council began, I therefore told Catholic journalists in Vienna that once it started, they should not wait to ask their bishops, but should inform the world of what was being said at the Council and not hesitate to criticize or press for answers whenever they thought it necessary. It was their duty, in the interest of both parties, to get the Church and the world to engage in dialogue. I also encouraged them to write about what ordinary people, especially the Catholic faithful, expected of the Council so that what began as a hope would not end in disappointment.

I am certain that the decision to inform the world of what was being debated at the Council set an excellent example. The fact that the entire Roman Catholic hierarchy and more than a hundred observers from other Christian denominations had gathered in Rome to review crucial spiritual issues in all openness at a time when the world seemed solely engaged in political or wordly matters (the Council convened from September 1962 to December 1965, at the height of the Cold War) was seen as a positive signal. The world realized the far-reaching implications and gave a nod of assent. The way in which public opinion propagated the Council exceeded all forecasts. Accomplished and committed journalists like Mario von Galli of the Swiss journal *Orientierung*, who covered the Council for the German-speaking world, Peter Hebblethwaite of the English Jesuit journal *The Month*, and Robert Blair Kaiser of *Time* magazine, to mention only three, connected the Aula of St Peter's with the outside world and 'transcribed' the topics that were being discussed, the debates that ensued and the often seemingly endless proposals and amendments into a language that the world could understand. This not only required an exceptionably observant eye and the ability to grasp overall connections quickly, but also a gift for asking the Church and the world the right questions at the right time and then commenting critically. It takes immense patience to accomplish such a feat, but also a great sense of humour – and the journalists concerned did a wonderful job. For over three years the Council was prime news worldwide, much of it positive. Even the Ecumenical Patriarchate's official newspaper, *Apostolos Andreas*, was full of praise, and the Greek Orthodox Church's newspaper, *Ecclesia*, wrote, 'At this Council the Catholic Church has shown that it is a different Church from the one we have known up to now.'

We connect the splendour and the glory of the Council with Pope John, but the spadework was left to Paul VI. He had to shoulder the burden of Vatican II. I think future generations will come to a more just appraisal of Paul VI's role at the Council, and appreciation of what he did will grow. For me he was the martyr of Vatican II. The death of Pope John in June 1963 left the Council in a precarious position. What would happen now? Who would succeed Pope John? And would whoever succeeded him proceed with the Council or break it off? All the Council Fathers and with them the entire Church waited in trepidation. My very modest room at the conclave was next to that of Cardinal Montini of Milan. On the very first day of the Council it soon became clear which way the wind was blowing and that Montini would be elected. That night he looked so downcast that I decided to drop in on him. When I told him that I, too, shared the general view that he would be elected the next day and was over-joyed, he kept trying to convince me that I was wrong. As we said goodnight he said, 'I am enveloped by com-plete darkness and can only hope that the dear Lord will lead me out.' When he was elected the next day, I feared he would say 'No', as has repeatedly happened at con-claves. But Montini said 'Yes' – albeit very hesitantly. He did not want to become Pope. From that moment on, however, it was more or less clear that the Council would go on. A few days later Paul VI declared his intention of continuing the Council along the lines that Pope John had conceived. Paul VI greatly admired his predecessor. He had not spoken much during the first session of the Council, but the little he had said showed that he was fully in favour of Church renewal. Although he did not convoke the Council or begin the reform process, he con-tinued it and saw it through. This was not easy, expecially for someone who, unlike John XXIII, did not have the charm to stir people with a single smile. But Paul VI had the tenacity, perseverance and will power to soldier on. And he also had that strength which comes from great humility to step back and make himself small when faced with an overwhelming task. The great work of Church renewal, however faltering, hesitant, inhibited and obstructed it may sometimes seem to us, would have crumbled if he had not persevered. The Council pro-ceeded, albeit with small, faltering steps – and at times it even came to a standstill – but there was no change in direction, and the aim was never lost sight of. Pope Paul picked up what his predecessor had triggered, and translated it into action.

I will never forget the solemn ecumenical service in St Peter's on 7 December 1965 which marked the end of the Council. I was one of a small group on the altar with Pope Paul VI. After asking the representative of the Ecumenical Patriarch of Constantinople to join him there, the Pope announced that the Papal Bull of 1054, which had declared the Great Schism between the Western and Eastern Church, was now null and void. I can still hear the thundering burst of spontaneous applause with which his announcement was greeted, and many of those present had tears in their eyes. For me this highlight signalled that the impulses set off by the Council were already at work. The crucial process of reception, that all-important part of any Church Council, which can take two generations and more, had begun.

2

Inner-Church dialogue

Even today, 40 years after the Second Vatican Council, the world and the Church remain two different entities, with little in common. In their everyday lives, most people, and that includes most Christians, compose their own moral standards, especially as far as sex, marriage, business or politics are concerned. This means that their consciousness is often split. A split of any kind, however, is always destructive.

There are two possible ways of contending with a negative development of this kind. One is for the Church to counter such disintegration by hardening itself against it, which would mean that it would be excluded and isolated from the world and would live a sect-like existence. The other is to follow in the footsteps of St Ignatius who said, 'I accompany everyone through their door, in order to bring them out through mine.' For the Church, this means accompanying the world in the ways of the world, escorting people in their lives and drawing level with the world – not in order to align itself with the world, however, but so that it can be fully present in it.

How is the Church to reassert its presence in the world, not only outwardly but from within? It must make itself

heard and above all felt – people must feel that it is close
at hand. And it must be worth seeing, worth being heard,
worth being conversed with. In the final instance that
means that it must be credible in civil society. That is
what Pope John XXIII meant by *aggiornamento*.

Dialogue between the Church and the world, however,
can only succeed if there is dialogue within the Church
itself. At the moment, regrettably, inner-church dialogue
would seem to have ground to a halt.

One of the Catholic Church's main problems today is
its style of leadership. This is a twofold problem. While
papal primacy is the chief stumbling-block ecumenically,
within the Catholic Church itself, the main problem is
the inflated Vatican bureaucracy, which has taken over
the tasks of the college of bishops.

When the Council was first called, the college of
bishops had very little say in determining Church policy.
I was on the Preparatory Commission, which was made
up chiefly of bishops and was supposed to prepare
possible subjects for discussion at the Council. I soon
noticed that a not inconsiderable number of Roman
bishops with strictly traditional views were determined
to stop any move forward. They were not interested in
Pope John's *aggiornamento* as they considered it a
danger to the faith. After all efforts to stop the Pope from
calling a Council had proved to be in vain, there was this
strong tendency within the Preparatory Commission to
quash the Council. A number of bishops from Western
and Central Europe, however, including myself, Cardinal Frings of Cologne and Cardinal Döpfner of Munich,
were aware of the huge expectations the announcement

of a General Council had kindled the world over. I did not hesitate. At the next Commission session I got up and voiced my fears openly. It could not be denied that one or other of the Commission was trying to influence individual activities in order to rein in discussion and restrict it to as narrow a field as possible, I told the members. Thus, on the eve of the Council, in October 1962, armed with my first-hand knowledge of the desire for reform, I was able to assure Austrian Catholics that the Council would not be a Council of yea-sayers. The bishops would speak out clearly and openly, and there would sometimes be hard words. Concern that the Council would be dominated by the curia, and that the bishops' wishes would not be able to prevail against curial routine, were unjustified. The bishops would speak as their responsibility before God and the Church commanded them.

And during the Council, episcopal collegiality worked. Bishops from all over the world got to know one another and were able to exchange views. The Council made it quite clear that the bishops are not the Pope's emissaries, nor are they here, as some maintain, to carry out the Pope's instructions. They are not to be regarded, the conciliar document *Lumen Gentium* (27) states, as vicars of the Roman pontiff (meaning the incumbent bishop of Rome), as they exercise a power which they possess in their own right. They are witnesses and teachers of the faith in conjunction with the Pope, in the name of Christ. According to Vatican II, the episcopal college should share the Pope's burden and responsibilities, not merely in word, but also in deed.

However impressive the relationship of the episcopal

college with the Pope at its head appeared at the Council, however, it was not clear how this co-operation was
to work in practice when the bishops had returned to
their far-flung dioceses in different parts of the world.
The Council did not go into how episcopal 'concern for
the whole Church' could be put into effect. The task was
left to the post-conciliar period, and a solution is still
outstanding.

Paul VI, who was particularly concerned about collegiality, envisaged that regular bishops' synods would
continue the collegiality we had experienced at the
Council. At the 1971 synod, for instance, he put the issue
of priestly celibacy up for debate and assured me personally beforehand that he would accept the bishops'
decision. At the time, the majority of bishops decided
in favour of keeping mandatory priestly celibacy for
Catholic priests in the Latin-rite Church, but the point
I am trying to make is that Paul VI was prepared to let
the bishops decide. He also took great pains to remodel
the advisory and controlling function of the curial authorities in order to bring them into line with the Council's
intentions. On the last day of the Council (7 December
1965), he improved the Congregation for the Doctrine of
the Faith's procedure, which used to be far more
inquisitorial.

The present Pope did not grow up in the Vatican. When
he became Pope he could only take note of the huge Vatican apparatus that he was confronted with in Rome. I
personally think he decided to choose a number of
experts and then left them to run it – and they, of course,
claim to speak in his name. Formerly the Pope even

occasionally noticed that this claim was not always quite accurate, but probably told himself that it was not worth his while to start an argument. Meanwhile, however, when one considers how much is still published in the Pope's name, I would say that it is highly improbable, not to say physically impossible, that all those documents can have been written by the Pope himself. That also, no doubt, accounts for the fact that certain issues, like mandatory priestly celibacy, for instance, have been blown up out of all proportion lately, as if the Church's survival dependend on maintaining the celibacy rule! Even Cardinal Ratzinger has admitted that too much paper comes out of the Vatican. On the other hand, one should not forget that Vatican bureaucracy is not homogeneous and that there are critical voices in Rome, too.

How the college of bishops could function as a body is not only a theoretical but also a practical question. There are various ways in which this could be realized, but the most important first step must be to accept that a change in mentality in this direction has taken place. Then we can go on to consider the two or three possible ways in which this could be put into practice. Dividing the Church into Patriarchates, as the former Archbishop of San Francisco, John. R. Quinn, and others have suggested, would be one solution, which suggests itself historically, moreover. I agree with those bishops who think it would be a good idea if the heads of the bishops' conferences were to meet regularly with the Pope every two or three years to discuss a number of specific subjects that are currently of particular importance.

This would enable the Pope and the bishops to get a broader, overall view of what was happening in the Church. They would be better informed and would find it easier to see things in the right perspective. The Pope would not, as has been the case at bishops' synods under John Paul II, ask the bishops to let him have their opinions and then word the final document himself, but would involve the bishops in the decision-making and allow them to participate in finding a final solution. They would thus share in the governance of the Church with the Pope, as the Council intended. Leadership problems in the Church can only be solved if the Pope shares the concern and responsibility for the whole Church with the bishops.

Particular attention should also be paid to subsidiarity within the Church. It helps us to get a clearer meaning of what collegiality entails, showing us that each bishop has unrestricted responsibility for his own field of competence. It also means that higher-ranking organizations should offer subsidiary ones help and support so that they can accomplish their own specific tasks. The principle of subsidiarity assures the independence, intitiative and strength of the individual versus the community, and also of small groups *vis-à-vis* larger ones. The laity, for example, should be entrusted with tasks that they can carry out as well as, or better than, priests.

The fact that the episcopal college has not been involved in governing the Church is directly linked with the current policy of episcopal nominations. One of the reasons for the present polarization in the Church, especially in the German-speaking world, is directly connected with the way in which bishops have been appointed in recent years. In the years after the Council it was easier for bishops to keep Catholics united. By allowing a certain amount of diversity, we were able to preserve a greater unity. Bishops' conferences spoke with one voice. That is not to say that the bishops did not have differences of opinion, but they were united in diversity. Unfortunately, this is no longer the case today. Nowadays we hardly know one another, except perhaps regionally.

There is widespread agreement that bishops should not be nominated by the Vatican alone, as has been the case for some years now, but that both the Vatican and the local Church should have a say in episcopal nominations. No one is against the Pope having the final word. Even in the Eastern-rite churches, which are in full communion with Rome, but where bishops are elected, each appointment is confirmed by the Pope. The local diocese always used to be involved in our Latin-rite Church, too, but then Rome became nervous. The Roman authorities thought that caution was called for as there was too much unrest in the Church and thus it was decided that it would be better for Rome to act alone.

A spate of episcopal nominations in Austria in the late 1980s and early 1990s, for example, were not at all an ideal solution. Luckily, so many in such a short time were pretty much of an exception as far as the world Church was concerned, but an unfortunate one all the same. These nominations have led to years of conflict and polarization in the Austrian Church.

Since 26 March 1995, moreover, when grave allegations of sexual abuse were first made against the then

Cardinal Archbishop of Vienna, Cardinal Hans Hermann Groer, many people, both inside and outside the Church, have lost trust in it. The Long Good Friday of the Austrian Church, as I called it at the time, and which caused me untold suffering, is proving very difficult to overcome. All of us in the Church are sinners. This is something the Church and everyone in it must always be acutely aware of and which we must admit openly. Allegations must be faced in the interest of the Church's credibility. In January 1984 Pope John Paul II told journalists that the Church was trying hard, and would try even harder in future, to be a 'House of Glass' where everyone could see what was happening and observe how it carried out its mission in faithfulness to Christ and the gospel message. Unfortunately it is still a long way from being a 'House of Glass' and is rightly criticized for its lack of transparency. We live in a media society, but it would seem that the Church has not yet learnt how to cope with this fact. An open Church in a media society cannot just find fault with others and never admit to its own mistakes. When enough time has passed to allow for an objective analysis, historians will have to go into what really caused the Austrian Church crisis. If we are to live together in a pluralist society, such an analysis is imperative.

We must try and re-create an atmosphere of trust. Vatican diplomacy used to be renowned for having its finger on the pulse of the times and being able to assess the trends in local Churches accurately in order to reach decisions that would both fulfil local needs and hopes, and at the same time benefit the whole Church. One can only hope that the Vatican will revert to its former tried and tested policy.

The rift between what the Church teaches and how people live their lives is perhaps most acutely felt in the so-called Western world. It is this rift which leads to heated discussions on issues like mandatory priestly celibacy, the role of women in the Church, birth control and Communion for remarried divorcees. When the Vatican responds 'from above', as it were, by publishing the Church's teaching on these issues, the Catholic faithful do not feel that it is they who are being addressed. The theological language in which the official documents are worded gives the impression of being impersonal and cold, and moreover sometimes smacks of arrogance. There is no trace whatsoever of any personal contact and the human-dialogue partner is missing and excluded. I fully understand the Vatican's fear that church unity could break apart, but there is no need to be discourteous. No one loses authority just because they are polite.

It is a case of preserving unity in diversity. For individual Catholics to feel that the Church is not some distant authority, but has their interests at heart and is close to them, continental and territorial awareness within the Church must be strengthened. This will require further deliberation and there is undoubtedly a certain risk involved. It will take time and will not be easy. One could, for instance, discuss whether a special solution of the celibacy problem should be considered for Europe or Latin America. The celibacy debate is understandable as mandatory priestly celibacy is not a dogma. It is often forgotten that we already have different solutions for this problem within the Catholic Church. The Eastern-rite Churches, which are in full communion with Rome, allow married men to become priests. The reason why Rome is set on maintaining the celibacy rule is because for a Pope from Poland it is inconceivable that a rule which has been in force for centuries, and which has proved its value – if indeed that really is the case – should be changed. I am convinced that the next Pope will permit the ordination of *viri probati*; that is, proven married men. Making celibacy optional for Latin-rite priests would solve certain problems, but others will arise. Within a short time we would probably be confronted with the problem of divorced priests. The human factor in the Church is always a great burden.

And of course we must continue to discuss the role of women in the Church – this is unique and of primary importance. Christianity has always insisted on the equality of men and women before God, but that does not mean to say that men and women are identical. On the contrary, I would say that they are radically different. Women can do many things that men cannot. God made man *and* woman. The sexes complement each other. It is my opinion that the Church would benefit greatly if gradually many more women were appointed to high postitions in the Vatican congregations so that they could bring in their unique viewpoints and experience. I am sure this will come, but in a 2,000-year-old institution it will take time and will be a slow process, just as it was in the secular world. Women did not become government ministers overnight.

There are two main obstacles to women's ordination

at the moment: tradition and ecumenical relations. In the Anglican Church, women's ordination almost led to a schism and the question of whether women should be ordained bishops is still hotly contested, not only by men but also by many women. One cannot change traditions from one day to the next. There is no doubt, moreover, that if the Catholic Church were to ordain women now, the Orthodox Church would withdraw from Catholic–Orthodox dialogue altogether. I am in close contact with many Orthodox churchmen and was only recently assured that that would be the case. That does not mean, however, that we must not continue to discuss women's ordination, and must above all listen carefully to what women themselves have to say on the issue.

The most tragic rift between official Church teaching and the great majority of Catholics occurred when Pope Paul VI's encyclical *Humanae Vitae* was published in 1968. I talked to Paul VI frankly about the encyclical beforehand and warned him that it would cause a multitude of problems, particularly the differentiation between 'artificial' and 'natural' birth control. Differentiating between the two in this way made it look as if morally nature could be outwitted by a trick. I have since been assured by countless Catholic doctors that in the long run this differentiation cannot hold medically. Paul VI reminded me that the encyclical only concerned the general norm, but my impression was that he did not really understand or realize that it would cause untold problems for Catholic families; in some cases heartbreaking problems, especially for Catholic women.

Humanae Vitae plunged the Church into a credibility crisis and the developments in the Church's teaching on sexual morality since have been tragic. Guidelines are certainly necessary, but the significance of the personal conscience must not be overlooked. Two months after *Humanae Vitae* was published, in October 1968, the Austrian bishops' conference, like several other bishops' conferences at the time, published a declaration, the so-called 'Maria Trost Declaration', emphasizing the significance of the sincerely informed conscience in the matter of birth control. I firmly reject recent accusations from certain ultra-conservative churchmen who say that the Austrian bishops' declaration threw people into confusion. As president of the Austrian bishops' conference at the time, I naturally discussed the text of the declaration with Pope Paul VI, and later also with Pope John Paul II. Neither raised any objections concerning the text, which they would have been obliged to do if it had contained any serious errors.

In their declaration, the Austrian bishops particularly emphasized the positive role model of marriage and responsible parenthood that Paul VI had underlined in his encyclical, but pointed out that the Pope had not spoken infallibly. It was conceivable that some Catholics might feel that they could not accept the complete ban on artificial birth control in their personal situation, the bishops said. Catholics who, after seriously examining their consciences and considering the matter unemotionally over a length of time, came to the conclusion that they could not accept the encyclical's teaching, were not sinning, the Austrian bishops concluded, but added that it was clear that they should refrain from spreading confusion among the faithful.

There is no doubt that we need clear principles and norms on Christian marriage and family life and that it is the task of bishops and priests to teach these norms. At the same time, however, those same bishops and priests are also bound to help those who are deeply distressed and burdened. Rules and regulations alone, however important they are, cannot always solve individual problems. In the final instance, birth control is a matter for the personal informed conscience. The Second Vatican Council defined the conscience as 'people's most secret core and sanctuary . . . There they are alone with God whose voice echoes in their depths.' It must be stressed, however, that the individual conscience is not a licence to do whatever one wants.

Even after almost 40 years, the real concerns of *Humanae Vitae* have lost none of their relevance. It is just unfortunate that their significance has been obscured by the construction of false antitheses. The key problems discussed, such as respect for the transmission of human life, the rapid increase in population, technical manipulation and responsible parenthood, are as important today as they were then. I have always been at pains to point to the positive role model of marriage and responsible parenthood that Paul VI described in *Humanae Vitae*. He himself emphasized that exclusion of the contraceptive pill was not a dogma and that the encyclical was not infallible. He cut out passages that referred to mortal sin and in no way suggested that absolution must always be refused. Unfortunately *Humanae*

Vitae will only be remembered as the encyclical in which the Pope banned the pill. One thing is certain – *Humanae Vitae* left an open wound. The Church must show greater flexibility and understanding on this issue and particularly on such a delicate subject as birth control; it must word its directives with utmost sensitivity and take care never to sound as if it is sending people into despair. One of the foremost and most urgent tasks of the next Pope will be to reopen the discussion on birth control.

The problem of whether remarried divorcees should under certain circumstances be allowed to receive Communion is similar. Again this is a question of possible exceptions to a general rule. Marriage is insoluble, but there are cases when a second marriage is not inevitably sinful. Once more, in the final instance, it is a decision of conscience. The important point for the Church is to admit that these issues are open wounds which must be discussed further.

In the past I often used to discuss the question of the individual conscience with Pope John Paul II. He showed great understanding but was inclined to emphasize the clerical aspect.

These are only some of the issues the next Pope will have to face. It is inconceivable in my eyes that anyone today would actually want to be Pope: the burden of responsibility has become far too great for one person. We must return to the decentralized form of leadership as practised in earlier centuries. One should not forget that although the Church is not a democracy, it has a long tradition of certain democratic elements. The Pope is elected. So are the heads of religious orders. For more than a thousand years bishops were elected by the faithful and then confirmed by the Pope, just as they still are today in the Eastern-rite Churches, which are in full communion with Rome. Returning to the earlier form of Church leadership will require a change in outlook which is a gradual process and cannot be decreed overnight, but that is what we must concentrate on. And we need to create such awareness together with the Pope and not against him, exactly as he himself requested in *Ut unum sint.*

Inner-church dialogue is not easy. We must not let those who are trying to run before they can walk, or those who, after venturing one timid step forward, immediately retract and take three steps back, confuse us. Neither the progressives nor the conservatives must be allowed to determine the Church's course. They must complement one another. Eliminating either or trying to prove that either one is based on a misunderstanding would deprive the Church of that dynamic tension which keeps it alive.

I have always favoured a middle course. That is why I would like to clarify my relationship to Opus Dei which has often been distorted in the media before closing this chapter on inner-church dialogue.

I first encountered Opus Dei in the 1950s. What impressed me was its emphasis on the importance of the laity in the Church, and that Opus Dei priests had to qualify in and practise a secular profession before they were ordained. Thus in 1957, one year after I became Archbishop of Vienna, I invited Opus Dei to Vienna. The first Opus priest to come was a certain Father Joaquin

Frances. When I heard that he had been Spanish national champion in highboard diving, somersault and springboard trampoline, I thought, 'Fantastic! That means that the Church is now not only present in St Stephen's Cathedral but also in the world of sport!'

I did not get to know the founder of Opus Dei, Escriva de Balaguer, until the Second Vatican Council. I and other bishops were often his guests at the Opus Dei centre in the Viale Bruno Bouzzi in Rome. Opus Dei was rarely mentioned at these gatherings, however. The main topic of discussion was the importance of the lay apostolate in the Church. Long before Vatican II, Escriva, who had travelled a great deal, realized how crucial the testimony of individual Christians in their everyday lives was for the Church in the world.

At the Second Vatican Council the Church spoke out authoritatively for the first time on the special vocation of the laity, saying they were called upon 'to make the Church present and fruitful in those places and circumstances where it is only through them that it can become the salt of the earth' (*Lumen Gentium* 33).

Even after the canonization of its founder in 2001, many people still regard Opus Dei with scepticism and mistrust, but this is nothing unusual. It is quite normal and understandable for new movements in the Church to be treated with reserve and questioned, as so many of them eventually vanish into thin air or decline into sects. There are several reasons why Opus Dei acquired such a negative image. One of the roots of inner-church criticism of Opus Dei was its structure. It was first modelled on a secular institute, but when it became a personal prelature, friction with the diocesan structures was almost bound to follow. People feared it would become a Church within the Church. Moreover, although it was primarily founded for the laity and only 2 per cent of its members are priests, it has sometimes given the impression of being 'priest-dominated'. Maybe some Opus priests put themselves too much in the limelight and overdramatized their role. It is also often rumoured that Opus Dei has great influence in the Vatican and is favoured by the present Pope. Gossip-mongering is a favourite pastime in the Church. Isolated occurrences tend to be generalized, moreover. But people have every right to worry about such rumours, especially the Catholic faithful. The reason why Escriva was beatified so soon, only seventeen years after his death, probably has more to do with the fact that the beatification procedures had been simplified and abridged shortly beforehand and his was one of the first procedures to come under the new regulations. Whether or not his seemingly hasty beatification was opportune at the time, however, is quite another matter. I personally would have given a little more thought to the impression such extraordinary haste was bound to make.

A further reason why many Catholics feel uneasy about Opus Dei is that so many of its members are in leading positions in politics, finance and even in armaments production where efficiency is imperative. There is always a certain danger that such people will put too much emphasis on performance in their religious lives, and that can easily lead to tension with those Catholics for whom an achievement-oriented mindset is completely foreign and which they find offputting and even 'un-Christian'. Too much emphasis on excellence gives the impression of being elitist. Opus Dei has also been accused of being too secretive and using cover-up tactics. Everyone in the Church has a right to discretion, but there must be no going back to the pre-conciliar mentality of keeping as much as possible secret, not so much because this might be seen as an attempt to conceal dubious activities, but because it could be interpreted as a sign that the Church was once again withdrawing into itself and closing its doors on a world it considered evil and antagonistic to God. Opus Dei has a perfect right not to make its financial sources public, especially as many Church organizations and movements do not do so either. But might it not be worth Opus Dei's while to set a good example on this point and rise above itself for the Church's sake?

A negative image, which Opus Dei certainly had in the past, is not easy to shake off and it would do well to take its critics seriously. I personally think that it has now established its place in the Church, especially since its founder's canonization, and I am glad. I do not think that those responsible in Opus Dei aim to make their particular form of spirituality the general norm. That would be naïve and counter-productive. The Church is in dire need of Christians who lead exemplary lives and bear witness to their faith, as many Opus Dei members do, but this does not mean that they, or members of any other movements in the Church, are to be regarded as a yardstick for measuring the 'Catholicity' of other Catholics. When, in a pluralistic world, Christians speak out openly about their faith and how they model their

34

lives on it because that is what they believe in, they must be very careful how they go about it. A great deal will depend on their tone of voice and their choice of words. It is only too easy to sound militant or fundamentalist, and they must always bear in mind that the history of Christendom is all too full of examples of how unenlightened, blind miltancy led to ruthless mockery of the Gospel message.

There has always been room for different cultures, languages, schools of thought and devotional forms in the Church, whose motto is 'unity in diversity', and all efforts to make it uniform have always been doomed from the start.

3

Ecumenical dialogue

How dialogue with persecuted Christians behind the Iron Curtain led to dialogue with our sister Churches in the East: it all began with an accident

Under Pius XII, all Church contact with the communist world ceased and any form of dialogue was repudiated. Although the idea of a crusade against communism did not originate with the Vatican, it was not rejected by it either.

The news that Cardinal Stepinac of Zagreb, who had spent many years in communist prisons and was then put under house arrest by Tito, had died, reached me on 10 February 1960. Under normal circumstances, I, in my position as Archbishop of Vienna, would naturally have attended his funeral. In my case, however, there was an added reason. I knew Stepinac from our student days at the *Germanicum*, the German College, in Rome. He was by far the best volleyball player the college had at the time, and as a freshman I had been in his team.

In 1960, the Austro-Yugoslav frontier was still part of the Iron Curtain which separated the communist world from the West, and therefore hermetically sealed for Catholic churchmen. I was convinced that I would never be granted a visa, but decided to apply in order to demonstrate publicly that I wanted to go. Totally unexpectedly and to my great surprise, I was informed only two days later that my application for a visa had been granted and that I could attend the funeral. By this time it was 12 February and the funeral was on the thirteenth. The roads were icy so we could not drive very fast. After spending the night in Graz, we had no difficulty in crossing the Yugoslav frontier in the early hours of the thirteenth. We had just passed the small town of Varasdin in Croatia when the car skidded and crashed head-on into an oncoming vehicle. My chauffeur was killed outright and my secretary and I seriously injured. I regained consciousness in the local hospital with serious head injuries and a broken jaw. The doctor in charge, who spoke German, and with whom I remained in contact for years afterwards, had found me a single room. It was tiny, with just enough room for a bed. The first thing I saw when I opened my eyes was a huge picture of Tito staring down at me from the wall at the end of my bed. I lay there for several days, more or less motionless, with nothing else to look at for hours except that famous photograph of Tito in his marshall's uniform. Was this accident perhaps in some way significant for my life, I asked myself. It was then that it occurred to me that the Archbishop of Vienna was both geographically and historically closest to the countries behind the Iron Curtain and should perhaps be doing more to help the persecuted Churches under communist rule. This thought continued to preoccupy me during the whole of my convalescence and in hindsight proved a crucial watershed in my life.

I began to consider what possiblities there were for the Archbishop of Vienna to make contacts with the Churches behind the Iron Curtain now that the aggressive phase of communism seemed to be over. Vienna should not just be a bridgehead from which one could reach Eastern Europe, I decided, but a bridge which would enable people from the East to visit the West and vice-versa. I did not see myself as a diplomat or a Church politician, however. My concern was first and foremost a pastoral one. The German word for pastor is '*Seelsorger*', which literally translated means 'carer of souls', and I felt it was my duty to show those who were being persecuted for their faith in these totalitarian countries that they had not been forgotten, and to find ways of alleviating their suffering.

When I was lying in hospital in Varasdin in 1960, the Vatican was still convinced that we must wait for communism to collapse before making any contact with the Eastern bloc countries, but already then the wait seemed endless.

I had met Cardinal Wyszynski, the Polish Primate, in Vienna three years previously. I will never forget that first meeting. It was midday on 7 May 1957, a particularly peaceful spring day, when I received a message from the Austrian border guards on the Czechoslovak frontier that Wyszynski had just crossed the Iron Curtain by train and would be passing through Vienna on his way to Rome. Little was known about the Polish Primate at the time, although his name had cropped up from time to time in the West in connection with the Polish Church's resistance to communism. The news that Wyszynski's train was speeding towards Vienna soon spread like wildfire and there was every reason to fear that he would immediately be surrounded by large crowds and an uncontrollable throng of journalists on his arrival in Vienna. And indeed it was not long before the first curious onlookers started gathering both at the terminal where the rare trains that crossed the Iron Curtain arrived in Vienna, and outside the doors of the Archbishop's Palace in the inner city. In order to spare Wyszynski having to confront a crowd of international journalists, I immediately decided to head north towards the Czech border by car and board his train at Gänserndorf, a town not far from Vienna. As I had not met him before, I introduced myself, and after welcoming him to Austria, invited him to continue his journey to Vienna in my car. The three bishops who were accompanying him could go on by train, I suggested.

The Cardinal was obviously taken by surprise. Two large, enquiring eyes in a very pale face studied me intently. On hearing that he would be surrounded by Western journalists as soon as he got out of the train in Vienna, however, he willingly accepted my offer. We got into my car and proceeded to drive to Vienna. I, too, was nervous and unprepared. In 1957 it still seemed almost a miracle that the Primate of Poland had just crossed the Iron Curtain by train. It would have been quite inconceivable for a Catholic bishop from Western Europe to visit Poland or even Hungary, which was just a short drive from Vienna. Little did I know then that I myself would be travelling to both these countries in the none-too-distant future.

We did not speak much in the car, but when we spoke, we spoke Italian. Outwardly composed and inwardly withdrawn, my guest kept looking out of the window and gave me the impression at the time that his thoughts were still very much in Warsaw and with his persecuted Polish Church. Today we know that only a few days previously, on 1 May, the Polish Communist Party Secretary, General Gomulka, and the then Polish Prime Minister, had spent hours with the Cardinal late into the night trying to 'prepare' him for his audience with Pope Pius XII, but had met with little success. The questions the Cardinal put to me as we drove through the Lower Austrian vineyards towards Vienna still stand out very clearly in my mind. As yet somewhat lost in thought, he suddenly asked, 'What do you suppose God has in mind for us? How does he envisage the future of the Church in communist countries? Where does the way ahead lie and when will we see the light at the end of the tunnel?' That was our first encounter. It made a deep impression on me, and our talks gave me much food for thought. In the years that followed we became close friends.

I soon noticed that Wyszynski had to wait several days for an audience with Pius XII when he came to Rome. He later discovered that the Vatican did not wholly trust him because he was in contact with the communist government. After several long conversations with the Pope, however, he was able to persuade Pius XII that he was completely trustworthy, and everything was smoothed out. Looking back, I am certain that that first encounter of mine with the Polish Primate in Vienna blazed a trail for the Vatican. Wyszynski was a pioneer. Long before the Vatican itself decided to make contacts in Eastern Europe, he began a dialogue with the Polish regime and thus set the first signal for a change of course in the Vatican's *Ostpolitik*.

John XXIII opens the windows to the East

The decisive turning point came with John XXIII. He did not invalidate what Pius XII had said as he was not a dogmatist, not even when it came to being anti-doctrinaire. He was interested in dialogue and believed in the positive effects of personal contacts. At one of my first audiences with him he spoke to me at length about his plans for dialogue with Eastern Europe. He encouraged me to make contacts with the Church behind the Iron Curtain and asked me to be a 'small cog in the wheel' of this attempt at *rapprochement* beween West and East. And although I was convinced that my role could only be a modest one, it was certainly a sea-change in my life.

Already in 1961, when Catholic–Orthodox dialogue had hardly begun, I spoke to Pope John XXIII of my wish to visit the Ecumenical Patriarch, Athenagoras I, whom I admired greatly. The Pope was enthusiastic and suggested I leave Rome for Istanbul immediately. The Patriarch welcomed me warmly. He greatly admired John XXIII. It was Athenagoras who once greeted a top Vatican official with those simple but dramatic words from the Prologue of St John's Gospel: 'There was a man sent from God, whose name was John.' (I am deliberately quoting from the authorized King James version as in my eyes the opening passages of St John's Gospel in this remarkable English translation are unsurpassed.)

Athenagoras was a man of outstanding intelligence and great faith. He had spent some time in the United States and was convinced that the Orthodox Churches could no longer remain isolated. We spent three days together in the Phanar during which time he assured me that for him personally papal primacy was not an obstacle for Christian unity. We parted as friends. Not long afterwards we had the opportunity to deepen our friendship when he came to Austria for medical treatment and spent several weeks not far from Vienna.

Pius XII's intransigence towards communism had triggered a violent anti-religious campaign not only in Hungary but also in other Eastern European countries. John XXIII was to change that radically. He used to speak to me at length about his plans for reconciliation with the Slav peoples. As Apostolic delegate to Bulgaria he had come to understand and love the Slav peoples and how important it was not to condemn them only because we did not approve of their political system, as they had a deep spiritual inheritance which they had not lost. He was convinced that a way must be found to work together in the interests of world peace.

It was at one of these first audiences with Pope John that he suggested I visit Cardinal Mindszenty in Budapest. Mindszenty had fled to the US embassy during the Hungarian uprising of 1956, and had lived there in isolation ever since. When I pointed out to the Pope that this would not be easy as it would mean my crossing the Iron Curtain, which was still an almost insuperable obstacle for a Catholic churchman at the time, Pope John said in that direct way he had, 'What is so difficult about it? Go to the railway station in Vienna, buy yourself a ticket to Budapest and just go!' It was not quite that easy, but the Vatican and Austrian authorities were able to get me a visa, and after successfully shaking off the media by changing my official schedule a few times, I succeeded in crossing the border by car and drove on to Budapest. I will never forget my first meeting with Mindszenty. I was shown up to the third floor of the US embassy where the cardinal was waiting for me. 'What does the Pope want me to do?' he asked with a worried look in his large, melancholy eyes, as he invited me into his small room, where he immediately turned on the radio full blast, as he was convinced the embassy was bugged. We conversed in Latin and, as I listened to the anxieties and hopes of this desperately lonely man who had suffered so greatly for his faith, I realized that my intention to make contact with the persecuted Church behind the Iron Curtain had been right. It was essential and a foremost duty of the Archbishop of Vienna to show Christians in communist countries that their fellow Christians in the West cared.

That was only the first of my many visits to Cardinal Mindszenty. I visited him regularly once or twice a year for the next eleven years or so. While the Council was on, I always took him the latest Council texts. He would thank me profusely and put them on his desk, but I'm not

sure he ever read them, as when I brought the conversation round to the Council on my next visit, he would
fall silent. He greatly admired Pius XII, was reserved
towards John XXIII, but had great respect for Paul VI.
The latter would have liked him to leave Hungary of his
own will and repeatedly sent me to Budapest to try and
persuade him to come to Rome. In 1971 Paul VI finally
persuaded him. After a short stay in Rome where he was
not happy, he spent the last three years of life in Vienna.
From the beginning I had and still have the greatest admiration for his courage. Already imprisoned for his faith
by the Gestapo in World War II, he then spent eight years
in communist prisons and a further fifteen years confined
to those two small rooms in the US embassy in Budapest.
He was a true martyr for the faith and uncompromisingly
loyal to the Pope.

Although it was Pope John who first sent me to Eastern Europe when he asked me to visit Cardinal Mindszenty, I was never, as many people mistakenly believe,
and as I have explained repeatedly (unfortunately, it
would seem, in vain), a Vatican diplomat or part of the
Vatican *Ostpolitik*. I never negotiated with government
officials or their representatives. That was always
exclusively the concern of the Vatican Secretariat of
State. The reason why it fell on me to visit Mindszenty
is a simple one. I happened to be the archbishop who was
both geographically and historically best suited for the
job. Once I realized, moreover, that it was possible for
me as Archbishop of Vienna to cross the Iron Curtain, I
was able to pursue the resolution I had made after my
accident in Yugoslavia, namely to make personal contact

with the persecuted faithful in Eastern Europe and do everything within my power to help them. My feeling that such personal contacts would strengthen the awareness that Christians on both sides of the Iron Curtain shared a common bond was soon confirmed. At the beginning, I was, of course, sharply criticized. My trips would enhance the status of the communist governments, people said, and Catholics in Eastern Europe would see them as a betrayal, a stab in the back. Nothing could have been more wrong. On each trip I witnessed how grateful Christians were that they had not been forgotten – that we had not written them off An Austrian head of government told me years later that my journeys to Eastern Europe had reminded Austrian politicians that they, too, had obligations to our neighbours in the East.

Vienna had been a place of dialogue with the Churches of the East for centuries, and although more than 50 years had passed since the collapse of the Austro-Hungarian monarchy in 1918, Austria still had a good reputation with the peoples of Eastern Europe. Thousands of Eastern Europeans were able to listen to its radio and TV programmes. It was, moreover, a neutral country – and that made it easier for an Austrian bishop to travel to communist countries than it would have been for a bishop from a Nato state.

Two weeks before the third session of the Second Vatican Council came to an end with the passing of the decree on ecumenism, I decided to found Pro Oriente, a local diocesan institution in Vienna to promote ecumenical relations between the Roman Catholic and the Orthodox and Oriental Orthodox Churches and resume a dialogue that had been broken off centuries ago. It was decided from the very beginning that Pro Oriente would not have any official contact with the Greek–Catholic Churches, which are in full communion with Rome. I wanted to avoid getting involved in century-old resentments which would only have made dialogue with the Orthodox Churches far more difficult; and anyway, the Greek–Catholic Churches were under the direct jurisdiction of the Vatican Congregation for the Oriental Churches.

There had been Orthodox communities in Vienna for several hundred years and the ecumenical climate was good. I was also keen to show how the principle of subsidiarity could be put into practice. The local Church, *ecclesia particularis*, is the place where the universal Church is at work in its fullness, and I thought it important to illustrate how valuable the work of a local Church can be. It is sometimes better to discuss certain matters at the local level first before they are taken up by the world Church. Pro Oriente was often able to set things in motion inofficially, which would have been unthinkable at the official, Vatican level. To begin with, I do not think it would have been possible to create a similarly friendly atmosphere in the Vatican for the first talks for centuries with our sister Churches in the East. The fears and animosities that had accumulated over the centuries would have proved too great an obstacle. We needed a forum outside Rome where preliminary ecumenical discussions could be held and we could above all get to know one another. I felt freer to pursue these aims in Vienna, where I bore the sole responsibility and was neither hampered by Vatican bureaucracy, nor a burden to the Vatican itself.

At the time my relations with the Holy See and the Secretariat for Christian Unity were excellent, and so we were able to proceed without constraint. Thus Pro Oriente began to hold regular consultations and encounters not only with the Orthodox Churches but also with the Oriental Orthodox Churches, always in co-ordination with the Vatican Secretariat for Promoting Christian Unity but with complete freedom on our part. Pro Oriente became the advance guard of the Vatican's outreach to our sister Churches in the East which began under Pope John XXIII. It was, as it were, the barometer for measuring the ecumenical climate, and, as the 1960s and 1970s were the halcyon days of ecumenism, Vienna soon became a much frequented bridge between East and West.

In 1967 I was able to visit Romania at the invitation of the Romanian Orthodox Patriarch, Justinian. It was the first time the communist authorities allowed a Roman Catholic cardinal to enter Romania and I was the first cardinal to pay a visit to an Orthodox Church in Eastern Europe. Relations between the Vatican and the Romanian Orthodox Church were strained, as the Greek–Catholic Church, which is in full communion with Rome, had been forcefully integrated into the Romanian Orthodox Church. All contacts with Rome had been broken off and the Romanian Orthodox Church had not sent observers to the Second Vatican Council. When the then president of the Pontifical Council for Promoting Christian Unity wanted to visit Romania, he was refused an entry visa. It looked as if any form of dialogue between the two Churches was blocked. Yet the Romanian Orthodox Church was not only the second largest autocephalous Orthodox Church after the Moscow Patriarchate, but played an important mediatory role between Moscow and Constantinople. It was my hope that if it were possible, at least on this first visit, to avoid discussing the highly delicate problem of the Greek–Catholic Church, I might be able to improve the ecumenical climate.

I was met at the airport by Patriarch Justinian and, to my great joy, Bishop Aron Marton of Alba Julia, the only Roman Catholic bishop still in office in Romania. After spending six years in communist prisons, Marton had now been under house arrest for the best part of ten years. I had especially asked to see him, and as the authorities did not want me to visit him in Alba Julia, he had come to Bucharest to meet me – or so I thought when I saw him waiting for me at the airport. It was only later that I heard the full story. As Marton was under house arrest, he would have had to apply to the communist authorities for special permission to come to Bucharest. After all he had been through at the hands of the regime, however, he had made it a principle never to ask the communist authorities for anything. The communists therefore brought him to see me by force. As soon as I heard this, I immediately protested to the authorities. A month later Marton was given back his identity card and his house arrest was lifted. From then on, for the first time in sixteen years, he was able to visit parishes and perform confirmations.

Ecumenical Dialogue

Patriarch Justinian and I arranged for an exchange of
theologians, and a year later he was able to visit
Vienna. At my invitation, he gave the sermon at St
Stephen's Cathedral on the feast of SS Peter and Paul (29
June), the traditional day for ordaining priests. It was not
as yet at all usual for bishops from our sister Churches
to give sermons at Catholic Masses, and many people still
considered it unorthodox at the time; but the response
on both sides was very positive and helped to boost con-
fidence and reduce mistrust. From then on I made a point
of inviting bishops who came to Vienna for Pro Oriente
consultations as my guests to give a sermon at St
Stephen's. During his stay in Vienna, Justinian told me
that in his eyes the decentralization that Vatican II had
prompted and the fact that local bishops' conferences
now had greater independence, had brought the Catholic
Church closer to the synodal constitution of the Orthodox Churches. Moreover, bilateral contacts like ours –
that is, between the Romanian Orthodox Church and the
Catholic Church in Austria – were so promising in his
eyes that they might lead the way to top-level Catholic–
Orthodox dialogue. I think there is little doubt that
the success of his visit to Vienna eventually led to an
improvement in ecumenical relations between the
Vatican and the Romanian Orthodox Church.

My relations with the Russian Orthodox Church go
back to the Second Vatican Council. I still remember how
surprised I was when, on the second day of the Council,
shortly after we had been told that the Ecumenical Patriarchate of Constantinople had declined to send observers
to the Council (due to a misunderstanding, it later turned

out), I suddenly bumped into the representatives of the
Russian Orthodox Church quite by chance in St Peter's.
The Holy Synod had decided to accept Pope John XXIII's
invitation and had sent two observers to the Council.
This was largely due to the influence of Metropolitan
Nikodim of Leningrad and Novgorod, who wanted to help
the Russian Orthodox Church break out of its isolation
and make it better known internationally. His experiences in Jerusalem, where he had spent three years and
had personally witnessed how great the animosities
between the various Christian denominations there
were, had deeply saddened him and made him long for
Christian unity. Nikodim was greatly impressed by
Pope John XXIII's encouragement of ecumenical
dialogue, but also by his deep faith and simplicity. He
had expert knowledge of the Catholic Church and had
visited Rome in 1963. In the years following the Council,
his biography of Pope John XXIII contributed greatly to
a better understanding between Rome and Moscow.

One of the Russian Orthodox observers at the Council was Archpriest Vitaly Borovoi, a distinguished
Church historian, who from 1969 represented the Russian
Orthodox Church at the World Council of Churches and
was a consultant to the Department of Foreign Affairs of
the Moscow Patriarchate. He was very impressed by the
welcome given to the observers at the Council and the
special attention paid to them by the Secretariat for Promoting Christian Unity. Borovoi became a close friend of
Pro Oriente when it was founded two years later and frequently attended its meetings. I also invited the leader
of the Russian Orthodox Church in Vienna at the time,

Metropolitan Filaret Denisenko, to the founding ceremony, and our Churches soon began to exchange visits. In the following years, Pro Oriente delegations went to Kiev, Leningrad, Zagorsk and Moscow, and Russian Orthodox theologians came to Vienna to speak at ecumenical symposia and round-table conferences. The main subjects of discussion centred on primacy, ecclesiology and conciliarity.

In 1974 Pro Oriente used its unofficial contacts with theologians who represented their Churches at panorthodox ecumenical conferences to invite them individually to an 'unofficial ecclesiological colloquium' entitled 'Koinonia' in Vienna. The subjects for discussion were unity in faith and the diversity of its expression, the ecclesiological consequences of the term 'sister Churches' and of the lifting of the anathema of 1054, and what the actual prospects of sacramental and canonical unity were. The conference was lent importance by the fact that the Vatican Secretariat for Promoting Christian Unity and the Ecumenical Patriarchate's centre at Chambésy helped to organize it, and many prominent theologians, including Professor Joseph Ratzinger, now Cardinal Ratzinger and Prefect of the Congregation for the Doctrine of the Faith, attended. In retrospect, I am convinced that the Koinonia colloquium was epoch-making. It is doubtful whether it would have been possible to embark on official Catholic–Orthodox dialogue six years later without it.

In 1976, on the tenth anniversary of the annulment of the Schism of 1054, Pro Oriente held a conference on 'Prognoses for the Ecumenical Future' which Ratzinger again attended. In a notable address which attracted considerable attention at the time, he said that exhaustive study of the Church's teaching and practice of papal primacy before the Great Schism could contribute decisively to reconciliation with Orthodox Christianity. The way in which Roman primacy was formulated and practised in the first millennium would suffice for reconciliation on this issue, Ratzinger emphasized. Rome did not require more.

In September 1980 I accompanied a Pro Oriente delegation to the Soviet Union. It was the first visit to the Soviet Union by an archbishop of Vienna and was undertaken on my own initiative. It was not an official visit but a pilgrimage to the Russian Orthodox, Armenian Apostolic and Georgian Orthodox Churches under Soviet rule. We had no contact with the Soviet authorities. I wanted to show these Churches that they had not been forgotten and how greatly we valued their friendship. My visits to Eastern Europe over the previous fifteen years had confirmed my conviction that personal contacts were of primary importance ecumenically.

We first visited Moscow and then Zagorsk, the spiritual centre of Russian Orthodoxy. We were welcomed by Patriarch Pimen, but our audience with him was short. I immediately noticed that the Russian Orthodox hierarchy had become more cautious *vis-à-vis* foreign visitors than they had been in previous years. Metropolitan Juvenal, the successor of Metropolitan Nikodim (who, two years previously, in 1978, had died quite unexpectedly at the age of 49 in Rome during an audience with Pope John Paul I), was a little more open than Patriarch

Pimen. He told us that there was a steady increase in the number of seminarists in Russia and that 900 people were now doing a correspondence course in religion. Atheistic literature was inadvertently having a positive effect on young people, moreover. Its concentration on purely worldly issues and all-too-noticeable ideological propaganda had heightened their interest in religious and spiritual issues, he said.

As I had presided over the Vatican Secretariat for Non-Believers for the past fifteen years and this was my first visit to the Soviet Union, I wanted to know whether the official Soviet attitude to religion had changed in any way now that 60 years had passed since the October Revolution, and how atheism was being propagated in the 1980s. I had long wanted to visit the Museum of Atheism in Leningrad as I had heard that the exhibits for the 'proof that there was no God' had become more sophisticated over the years. I therefore decided to slip away on my own one evening while we were in Moscow and take the night train to Leningrad. I had hoped to remain incognito but unfortunately I must have been under observation, as when I got off the train in Leningrad the next morning, a Russian Orthodox priest whom I had not met before was waiting for me on the platform. (Not long afterwards he became the present Russian Orthodox Patriarch, Alexis II, and a good friend of Pro Oriente!) After he had introduced himself, we proceeded to the museum which was then still housed in the famous Kazan Cathedral. The director had obviously been informed that a Roman Catholic cardinal was coming to visit his museum as he immediately offered to give me a synopsis of the history of religion in the Soviet Union. I declined as tactfully as I could, saying I was far more interested in the exhibits which proved that there was no God. He seemed somewhat disappointed and a little nervous, but proceeded to show me a number of exhibits including an enormous Foucault pendulum which was supposed to prove that gravity, not God, was the force that held the planets in orbit. I had a distinct feeling that the poor man was embarrassed and fully aware that such arguments were hardly likely to convince me, but I did my best to murmur 'Oh, I see' as genuinely and gently as I could.

Back in Moscow I was able to hold Mass in a Catholic church but heard later that some Catholics had been prevented from attending and that a camera had been installed to photograph those entering the church.

From Moscow we flew to Soviet Armenia, where we were warmly welcomed by the Patriarch of the Armenian Apostolic Church, Vasken I. I had already received an invitation from him several years previously but, just as I was about to leave, the Soviet embassy in Vienna informed me that the visit had been cancelled. The Patriarch 'regretted', but my visit was 'not welcome', the message said. Shortly afterwards I discovered that the Patriarch had been as surprised as I was when he heard that my visit had been cancelled. We were both overjoyed that this time I had been permitted to come. It was possible to talk far more freely in Armenia than in Moscow, perhaps because Yerewan is more than 2,000 kilometres (1,242 miles) from the Russian capital. Vasken I spoke German fluently, moreover, and not only came to visit us in Vienna a few weeks later, but sent one of his young priests to study at the Vienna seminary. From Yerewan we continued to Tbilisi, the capital of Georgia, where we were equally warmly welcomed by members of the Georgian Orthodox Church.

We attended Orthodox and Armenian Apostolic liturgies in all three countries. I was asked to bless the faithful and got the impression that people were genuinely moved that we had come so far to show that they could count on our friendship. Some even had tears in their eyes. The high proportion of elderly women in church, especially in Moscow, was particularly striking. I can still see a seemingly endless chain of babushkas, with their different coloured kerchiefs, lighting and passing thin yellow candles to each other from the entrance, where one could buy them, right on up through the cathedral to the candlesticks at the foot of the iconostase in front of the altar during an evening liturgy we attended in Moscow. In Austria little old ladies who never fail to buy and light a candle when they enter or leave church are often spoken of somewhat disparagingly as 'candlelighting womenfolk' ('Kerzlweiber'). We should not underrate them. I was often reminded of them in the years to come. On my tours of Eastern Europe after the demise of communism so many young people told me that it was their grandmothers who had baptized them, often secretly, and had said their prayers with them at night when they were children. It was largely due to those grandmothers that Christianity survived at all under so many years of communist rule. In Western Europe, too, especially in Catholic countries like Austria, Italy and

Spain, the congregation nowadays often consists mainly of women, many of them elderly. Most parishes could not manage without their devoted service. As Christian communities continue to shrink in our increasingly secularized, multicultural societies, I am convinced that these women, and indeed women in general, will play a key role in passing on the faith.

Eight years later, in 1988, I again accompanied a Pro Oriente delegation to the USSR. We had been invited to attend the millennium festivities of the Baptism of the Kiev Rus': that is, the one-thousandth anniversary of the Christianization of Russia. Members of our delegation took part in the Russian Orthodox Council at Zagorsk as observers. It was on this occasion that we sent 500 copies of Metropolitan Nikodim's biography of Pope John XXIII, which Pro Oriente had published in Russian, as a gift to all the members of the Council and to the spiritual academies for distribution to their students and seminarians.

Breakthrough in the dialogue with the Oriental Orthodox Churches

The Oriental Orthodox Churches (that is, the Armenian–Apostolic Church, the Coptic Orthodox Church, the Ethiopian Orthodox Church, the Syrian Orthodox Church and the Malankara Orthodox Syrian Church in India) are five independent Churches which are in full ecclesiological and sacramental communion with one another and together have 25 to 30 million faithful worldwide.

Their rejection of the christological definition made at the Council of Chalcedon in AD 451 led to a schism.

Between 1971 and 1988 Pro Oriente held five non-official ecumenical consultations in Vienna at which Oriental Orthodox and Catholic theologians discussed those theological issues which had caused the schism 1,500 years previously. Already at the first such consultation, which was almost exclusively devoted to christology, a significant breakthrough was made. The Dean of the Coptic Orthodox seminary in Cairo, Amba Shenouda, who only a few weeks later became the Coptic Pope Shenouda III, came up with what has since become known as the 'Vienna Christological Formula' which defined the two natures of Christ in a way that was acceptable to both the Oriental Orthodox Churches and the Catholic Church. Two years later, in 1973, this formula was officially accepted by both the Catholic and the Orthodox Coptic Church and incorporated into the official Common Declaration signed by Pope Paul VI and Pope Shenouda III in the Vatican. An ancient christological dispute, which led to centuries of mutual isolation, vilification and mistrust, was thus substantially resolved. In the years that followed, Pope John Paul II signed similar declarations with the other Oriental Orthodox Churches.

Personal contacts played a particularly important role at these five Vienna consultations which were a first attempt, after 1,500 years, to resolve the controversial and delicate theological issues which had led to a schism.

In 1975 Pope Shenouda invited me and a Pro Oriente delegation to Cairo where I spent a week as his guest.

Just as I had stayed with a Parsee family when I accompanied Pope Paul VI to Bombay in 1964, I was able this time to stay with a Coptic family in Cairo which gave me an opportunity to get to know how Coptic Christians live. I have always found it regrettable how little many Christians know of one another. On the Friday, which is a Muslim holiday in Egypt, Pope Shenouda asked me to accompany him to the Friday evening meditation at St Mark's, the Coptic cathedral in Cairo, where he holds a weekly Communion service followed by discussions, a regular ceremony he introduced years previously when he was a young bishop. I was asked to say the homily and was surprised to find the cathedral packed to overflowing, above all with young people. In the course of the week we were also taken on a pilgrimage to Wadi El-Natrun, one of the oldest Christian monastery complexes in the Scetis Desert which goes back to the fourth century, and to Upper Egypt which was then 80 per cent Christian. With the help of my Coptic hosts, I was able to make contact with the young churches in Africa. My visit was important insofar as it drew worldwide attention to the situation of the Coptic Church, a minority Christian Church in a Muslim country, at a time when the influence of Islam was beginning to increase. It was also a public gesture of the Church's solidarity with a sister Church. I was also able to visit the vice-rector of Al Azhar, where I had given a lecture ten years previously, and discuss possiblities of renewing Christian–Muslim dialogue, especially among young people.

It is one thing for theological commissions to reach agreement, but quite another to ensure that news of the new insights gained gets through to the ordinary faithful and are understood by them. Theological consultations do not make spectacular news and are rarely reported by the media. Thus documents keep being published, but as the theological language and the historical connections are not easily understood by ordinary people, prejudice and mistrust remain.

In order to inform a broad spectrum of believers of the breakthrough that had been achieved at the Vienna consultations, Pro Oriente held a Middle East symposium in Egypt in 1991. It was the largest ecumenical gathering that had ever been held in the Middle East up to then, and one of the most successful examples of how ecumenical progress can be disseminated. Again at the invitation of the Coptic Pope Shenouda III, bishops, priests, theologians and a large number of lay persons from all the Oriental Orthodox Churches, the Eastern and Latin-rite Catholic Church, but also from the Anglican and Lutheran Churches, gathered at Wadi Natrun where they spent three days discussing the agreements that had brought to an end 1,500 years of theological misunderstanding. There was ample opportunity for personal encounters and discussions, and one could feel that the unity in diversity that all Christians should be aiming at. Prayers were said in Coptic, Arabic, Syrian, Armenian and Latin, and, after an ecumenical Vesper, I was touched to find myself surrounded by large numbers of Coptic Christians who all wanted me to bless them. They were obviously far less prejudiced against Roman Catholic cardinals than some theologians were and still are. After the symposium was over, we were invited to

Cairo where Pope Shenouda again asked me to accompany him to the Coptic cathedral, this time to attend the weekly catechesis he holds for 5,000 of his faithful every Wednesday evening.

Meanwhile, news of the ecumenical breakthrough that the Vienna Christological Formula had achieved spread, and the Pro Oriente statutes were expanded to include those Churches that had split from the Church before the Councils of Chalcedon and Ephesus. One of them, the Assyrian Church of the East, is traditionally said to have been founded by the Apostles Thomas and Bartholomew, and its liturgical language is still akin to Aramaic, the language Jesus spoke. Its schism with the Catholic Church goes back to the Council of Ephesus (431) which condemned the teaching of Nestorius of Constantinople, the spiritual father of the Assyrian Church. In 1990 Mar Aprem of Tichur was the first Assyrian bishop to visit Vienna. His memorable address, entitled 'Was Nestorius a Nestorian?', was a revelation to many of his audience, as the Assyrian Church had up to then been at the fringe of ecumenical interest and very little was known about it in Europe.

In June 1994, Pro Oriente was able to bring together all nine Churches of the Syriac tradition in Vienna, irrespective of their denominational affiliation. This included the Assyrian Church of the East, the Chaldean Church, the Maronite Church and both the Syro-Malabar and Malankara Catholic Churches of India. The presence of observers from the Pontifical Council for Promoting Christian Unity and of the Middle East Council of Churches at this first-ever meeting of all the Churches of the Syriac tradition from the Middle East, India and the diaspora in Europe and the New World underlined the importance of the Vienna consultation which has since become known as the first 'Syriac Dialogue'. It resulted in the signing of a Common Christological Declaration by Pope John Paul II and Mar Dinkha IV, the Catholicos-Patriarch of the Assyrian Church of the East, on 11 November 1994 in Rome. The influence which the 'Vienna Christological Formula', which was so successful in the agreement with the Oriental Orthodox Churches, had on this declaration cannot be overlooked. Both declarations prove how important it is to express our common witness of the faith in simple, contemporary language. As Pope John Paul II has emphasized, certain confusions and schisms in the past only arose because of differences in terminology and culture.

Ecumenical dialogue since the demise of communism

With the demise of communism in 1989–90, ecumenical dialogue entered a new and very turbulent phase. As they were often small oases of freedom and strongholds of resistance, the Churches in communist countries were naturally regarded as the state's number one enemy. The silent collapse of communism gave rise to great hopes in the West. Churches that had survived persecution and risen up out of the catacombs would surely lead to a Christian Renaissance in East and West. Bitter disappointment soon set in, however. The West was disappointed because new forms of exteme nationalism and a mistrust of all things Western soon filled the vacuum that communism had left, and the East was disappointed because the longed-for new order proved exceedingly painful and very difficult to achieve. Both sides were deeply disillusioned. After years of separation, East and West no longer understood one another. I will never forget one of my first meetings with Czech priests. Bishop Miloslav Vlk of Budejovice, now Cardinal Vlk and Archbishop of Prague, had invited me to talk to his priests on the Second Vatican Council. They were all elderly men – the youngest was 59. They were listening very attentively to what I had to say, but I could detect no sign of any reaction in their faces; no response was forthcoming. Deeply disturbed, as this had never happened to me before, I asked Bishop Vlk afterwards whether perhaps I had not made myself clear or done something wrong. His answer showed how little even I, who had had so many contacts with churchmen behind the Iron Curtain for years, knew what it had been like to live under communism. All the priests I had been talking to, Vlk said, had spent 20 to 30 years confined to their parish houses in complete isolation. In order not to compromise others, or get into political difficulties themselves, they had soon learnt never to give the slightest sign of recognition when they passed someone they knew in the street, even, or especially, when they passed their own parishioners. As there were spies everywhere, it was better to remain inconspicuous. Over the years, this forced isolation had changed their personalities. They had distanced themselves from everyone –

deliberately at first, but soon also unconsciously by way of self-defence. That was the first time that I fully grasped how deeply the communist system had damaged people. Paroles like 'The Party is always right' and 'Class enemies must be unmasked' had had their effect. They had destroyed the individual soul. As Bishop Vlk explained, it would take a long time for the 'deformed hearts' of these priests to heal.

I realized that in order to heal these scars, building bridges between East and West was more necessary than ever, especially now that the first euphoria after the fall of the Iron Curtain had evaporated. Far too few people in the West were really aware of how greatly communism had changed people in Eastern Europe. I set myself the task of devoting my remaining years to this challenge.

After the demise of communism, the Churches in former Eastern Europe were confronted with a number of new problems. The Catholic Church was faced with the problem of priests and bishops who had been clandestinely ordained in the underground and whose ordinations were not always easy to confirm. The individual Orthodox Churches seemed to go their separate ways. Certain sections of the Russian Orthodox Church had a deep aversion to the West which it held responsible for bringing rationalism, the belief in science and technology as a substitute for religion, and Marxism, which had led to the Russian Revolution, to the East. Such people were convinced that the West had only negative influences to offer. Other Orthodox Churches were faced with the difficult problem of coming to terms with their own past and with accusations that many of their priests and bishops had allegedly collaborated with the communists. The Orthodox Churches were not prepared for freedom and were faced with substantial material and spiritual challenges. The worsening of relations was partly the fault of Westerners. We very much gave the impression of considering ourselves superior and appeared on the scene as the rich uncle from the West, which was galling to our fellow Orthodox churchmen. It was wrong for Christian denominations to go to Russia with the aim of converting people. It was perhaps well meant, but appeared to be arrogant and presumptuous.

The attitude towards Catholicism, not only of the Russian Orthodox Church, but of the Orthodox Churches in general, became increasingly negative. Two problems were, and still are, particularly delicate – the restoration of the Greek–Catholic Church in West Ukraine and the readmission of the Catholic Church on former Soviet Union territory. The appointment of Catholic bishops who were of necessity foreigners, and later the Vatican's decision to establish dioceses on what was considered Orthodox territory, intensified the accusations of proselytism. When I accompanied a Pro Oriente delegation to Moscow in 1991, it was immediately obvious that the climate had worsened considerably. My long-standing contacts and Pro Oriente's mediatory reputation stood us in good stead, however. We were received by the Russian Patriarch, Alexis II, and also by Metropolitan Filaret in Minsk and were thus able to get an inside picture of the difficulties that were developing both in Russia and in the Ukraine. We must take accusations of proselytizing very seriously. Re-establishing pastoral care for

Catholics in Russia can have only one aim – to reach those who come from Catholic backgrounds. I think it is worth recalling Patriarch Alexis II's words in the preface he wrote for the 1993 edition of *One Thousand Years of Christian Russia* published by Pro Oriente:

> We are open to all those who come to us with pure intentions and are not practising open or hidden proselytism. We value and have the greatest respect for the ecumenical initiatives undertaken by the Pro Oriente Foundation and its concern to resolve inter-confessional conflicts in the interest of peace. This is of particular importance in connection with the revival of Greek–Catholic church structures in the West Ukraine.

Two visits to Lviv in 1993 and 1994 followed, in which we were able to sound out the exceedingly confused situation there and make first attempts at mediation.

In 1997, on the eve of the Second Ecumenical Assembly in Graz, Patriarch Alexis II came to Vienna on an official three-day visit. It had been hoped that he would meet Pope John Paul II at Heiligenkreuz Abbey outside Vienna, but the Holy Synod of the Russian Orthodox Church had cancelled the meeting. I had met the Patriarch in Munich and we had driven on to Vienna alone in my car. I distinctly got the impression that he had a personal interest in meeting Pope John Paul II as a gesture of reconciliation, but could not act without the approval of the Orthodox Holy Synod. He again confirmed that certain sections of the Russian Orthodox

Church had a deep aversion to the West and were strongly opposed to any *rapprochement* between Pope and Patriarch. I was reminded of my visit to the Serbian Orthodox Church in 1993 shortly after the Balkan War. While I got the impression that I was genuinely welcome in Serbia and the students I talked to at the Serbian-Orthodox theological faculty were really interested in Vatican II, the ecumenical movement as we understood it in Western Europe was foreign to them and was seen as a Western European concern. I was clearly given to understand that the Serbian-Orthodox Church had no interest in attending the Ecumenical Assembly in Graz.

The only way in which we can overcome such difficulties is to proceed in that spirit of love, mutual respect and humility which helped the pioneers of the ecumenical movement to reconcile their differences in the past. We must learn to respect not only each other's historical past, but also the the rhythm of each other's hearts. The restoration of Christian unity does not mean going back to the Christian Church of the first millennium as if the conflicts that separated us had never occurred: that would be impossible. Each of our Churches has meanwhile acquired its own history and traditions which cannot be eradicated. We must first of all make every effort to avoid expressions, judgements and actions which are not truthful or fair when we refer to each other, as the Vatican II decree on ecumenism says. In small steps we must then try to remove the obstacles which still separate us. Impatience of any kind is quite out of place. Ecumenism moves slowly and in stages, never in leaps. Maybe we are going through a

more difficult period at the moment than the one immediately following Vatican II, but one certainly should not
talk of stagnation. When I think of what the Church was
like when I was young, I can only marvel at what we have
achieved. A year or two ago I was invited to Vespers and
to address the congregation at the Anglican church here
in Vienna and no one thought this anything out of the
ordinary. We have come a very long way indeed, and there
will be no going back, I am sure of that. It is a matter of
demonstrating the positive forces that genuine ecumenism can rally in a largely secularized, multicultural
society in which many people seem to have lost their
bearings. A growing feeling of consensus among the
Christian denominations strengthens the longing for
harmony, peace and justice for the whole of humankind.

4

Christian–Jewish dialogue

Christian–Jewish dialogue is especially dear to my heart, and I am deeply grateful that I have been allowed to live long enough to witness the progress it has made over the last 40 years.

I still remember how shocked I was as a young priest and scripture scholar in the early 1930s when I realized for the first time that certain passages in the Good Friday liturgy had for centuries been misunderstood, and had encouraged Christians to spurn Jews; but the strange thing is that neither I, nor many of my fellow churchmen or theologians, went further into the matter at the time. The question that continues to prey on my mind is why it took the Church so long, until the Second Vatican Council in fact, to refute and openly oppose Christian anti-Judaism.

From the early Middle Ages right up to the mid-twentieth century, the misinterpretation of certain passages in the New Testament played a decisive role in prejudicing people against Jews and therefore share, if only indirectly, the responsibility for countless pogroms and in the end for Auschwitz. I am convinced that openly admitting this guilt to the Jewish people is not a sign of weakness but rather of a strength of faith. Perhaps the fact that I experienced the rise of Hitler and the war years in Austria as an Austrian priest made me particularly sensitive to the fact that the Church shared the guilt for the shoa and all the problems connected with it.

Christian–Jewish dialogue has made great strides since Vatican II at the top, intellectual level. There is, however, still a great deal to be done at the grass-roots level. As an Austrian Catholic of the war generation I have been deeply disturbed in recent years to see arguments resurfacing that I thought had been dealt with once and for all. I have described my war experiences in some detail below in the hope that they will help to build bridges where they still need to be built. Reality is complex and has many dimensions: it cannot be seen in terms of black and white.

In that part of Lower Austria where I was born and spent my childhood years, long before World War I, there were not many Jewish families, but I do remember my mother taking me to the local grocer's shop and explaining that the owners were not Christians but Jews. There was nothing at all negative about the way she said this, however. She was stating a fact – namely, that some people are Christians and some are not. I never heard any derogatory remarks about Jews as a child, or that there was any hostility between Jews and Christians.

After finishing high school in 1927, I accepted a scholarship to the Gregorian in Rome where I studied philosophy and theology. It was my interest in non-Christian religions – my special subject was Zoroastrianism in Ancient Persia, which I studied at the Biblical Institute

– that first brought me into contact with the Old–Oriental World, and that in turn helped me to deepen my knowledge of the Bible, particularly of the Old Testament.

I was ordained in Rome in 1933. I have already mentioned how disturbing I found the pre-conciliar Good Friday liturgy as a young priest. The Latin *Oremus et pro perfidis Judaeis* was translated in the Roman Missal as 'Let us pray also for the perfidious Jews', but the Latin word *perfidus* can have either a neutral or a pejorative meaning. Over the centuries, the pejorative meaning had prevailed. Most people, including most Christians, were, of course, quite unaware of this semantic background. 'Perfidious' was naturally assumed to mean 'treacherous'. I was shocked when I realized this, but in the country district in Lower Austria to which I was moved a year after my ordination, there were no Jews and I had no Jewish friends or acquaintances, so did not go into the matter further at the time. In retrospect, I realize with shame that I should have done.

I had been away from Austria for six years and meanwhile Hitler had found many sympathizers, chiefly because he was creating jobs at a time when Europe was going through a catastrophic depression and millions were unemployed. Many Austrians were thankful that he was providing them with enough to eat and vouched for order and prosperity after years of unrest and poverty. And then there were those for whom Bolshevism was the apogee of evil. Many Catholics, including a considerable number of the clergy, initially sympathized with the Nazi cause because they regarded Hitler's Germany as a bulwark against communism.

In the small Lower Austrian town of Scheibbs where I was a curate in 1938, the Nazis concentrated their attacks on Catholics who refused to go along with their racist ideology, and we priests in our cassocks were often openly scoffed at and called names in the streets. I was in Scheibbs when the German Army crossed the border and occupied Austria on 12 March 1938. I still remember how deeply shocked I was on leaving the parish house next morning, after a relatively sleepless night, to find swastikas hanging from all public buildings and many private houses as well. There is no denying that hundreds of thousands of Austrians, including many Catholics, cheered Hitler as he drove through Austria; but from my own experience I also know that a far greater number stayed at home and wept.

A few months later I was appointed cathedral priest in St Pölten and at the same time began teaching religious education at a secondary school there. I had only been teaching a month or two, however, when the headmaster called me into his office and curtly informed me that my services were no longer required. Times had changed, was the way he put it, and religious education was no longer of interest. I had by this time studied Nazi ideology in detail and was familiar with works such as Houston Stewart Chamberlain's *The Foundations of the Nineteenth Century* and Alfred Rosenberg's *The Myth of the Twentieth Century*, both of which had a profound influence on Nazi thinking. Chamberlain's emphasis on the racial superiority of the so-called Aryan element in European culture, his belief that Germany was the nation best suited to establish a new European order, and above all that the Jews were 'aliens' in Europe, greatly influenced German nationalism and Hitler's dreams of a thousand-year Reich. After the collapse of the Austro-Hungarian Monarchy in 1918, the idea of Austria becoming a part of this Greater Germany grew in popularity in Austria. When Hitler came to power, the so-called 'German Nationals', who were extremely xenophobic, were, of course, exultant. I often think that their particular brand of xenophobia was probably the reason why anti-Semitism was so rabid in certain circles in Austria.

I soon realized that the Nazi regime was threatening all spiritual values. Under the pretext of giving liturgy instruction, which was still officially allowed, I continued to meet my pupils in the cathedral sacristy. We called ourselves the 'Young Church' and our 'lessons' consisted chiefly in discussing the burning issues of the day. By this time of course anti-Semitism and the Jewish problem worried me deeply, but it was not until all Jews were forced to wear the Star of David, known as the 'yellow star', that it first fully dawned on me that Nazi persecution was primarily, and by this time virulently, aimed at the Jews.

As cathedral priest I was exempt from military service. By 1940, the Gestapo had become suspicious of our meetings, so we would often meet in the woods. In order to put the Gestapo off our tracks, I would cycle round the country roads first – wearing a swastika armband and a pair of highly polished officers' boots that someone had got hold of somewhere – and then join the others after dark. I knew that I was endangering not only myself but also my pupils, but the danger that these young people would settle with the situation was greater. It was crucial, in my eyes, to point out to them how anti-Semitic and full of hatred Nazi ideology was. After praying and singing together we would discuss the situation we were in and how we could help those who were in imminent danger of arrest by the Gestapo. People of all kinds came to the cathedral, most of them seeking help (Gestapo officials would also call, probably just to see what we were up to), and I often knew where people were in hiding and where help was needed most. Sometimes some of us managed to listen to the BBC and we were able to share the news. In the course of time several of the boys were called up. I was able to keep up a correspondence with them at the front. Luckily we were careful not to give anything away in our letters, as after the war the postwoman confessed to me that she had had to take all my letters to the Gestapo headquarters to be censored. After the war I published these letters. They were written by mere boys as they lay wounded at the front or on their deathbeds. I was interrogated several times but was able to talk my way out. One day, however, I was summoned to the notorious Gestapo headquarters at the *Morzinplatz* in Vienna. I was innerly convinced that my chances of being released this time were pretty slim and that I would be sent to Dachau. The interrogations lasted all day. At one point the officer conducting the interrogation left the room for a moment. I saw a list of people due to be arrested on his desk and quickly pocketed it. It was an automatic reaction rather than a 'heroic' one. I still do not know to this day why I was released late that night. Perhaps the war had reached a stage when the interest in cases like mine had waned. When I got back to St Pölten I quickly sent some of my pupils to warn the people on the list I had taken.

In the last months of the war St Pölten was caught between the German and the Russian fronts. Our bishop had given orders that we priests were to remain in the cathedral and give people whatever help we could. Bombs rained on St Pölten as it was an important railway junction, and endless columns of refugees passed through ahead of the Russian armies. There was room for 600 people in the cathedral cellars, and we priests, dressed in our cassocks and wearing Red Cross armbands, tried to help where we could. As I could speak Russian, I now found myself protesting to the Russians at the way our women were being treated. It was a terrible time. The suffering I witnessed on all sides in the last months of the war had a formative influence on the rest of my life. Sometimes, late at night, we priests would discuss the future of the Austrian Church. At the time of the Habsburgs the Austrian Church had leant on the Emperor, and later, after the Peace of Saint Germain, on the Christian-Social Party. Now, under Nazi rule, for the first time in its long history, it was left to its own defences. It was already clear in my mind that those of us who survived the war must keep the Austrian Church out of party politics in future. Even if the idea met with opposition, the Church would have to be above politics and become the nation's 'conscience'.

When the war was finally over, Austria lay in ruins. The spiritual and material devastation wrought by seven years of Nazi rule was appalling. People's first instinct in 1945 was to survive. I can remember how loath people were to talk about what they had experienced during the war. Most Austrians tried to forget and concentrated on rebuilding the country. This is humanly understandable but it also explains why coming to terms with the past proved so difficult for them. There was a general fear that ghosts from the past could poison the present and the future. Some, perhaps even many Austrians, had reason to feel guilty, and many were consumed with guilt. But there is no such thing as collective guilt: one cannot condemn a whole nation. From today's perspective I can understand the young who reproach the war generation for not having done enough to oppose Hitler. But I, as one of that older generation, would not dare accuse those who kept silent of cowardice or collaboration. I had no family, but those who did risked that their families would be held liable for any form of resistance on their part. I suppose I, too, could be accused of not having done enough. After all, a considerable number of Austrian priests died for their faith under the Hitler regime – either under the guillotine or in concentration camps. I don't know what I would do if I were asked to my face why I did not do more to oppose Hitler. Maybe I would just remain silent. I am deeply convinced, however, that anyone who asks that question should first of all ask themselves if they would have had the courage to do more under the circumstances.

In retrospect, no doubt, we as Christians should also apologize for the errors committed by church leaders at the time. Cardinal Theodore Innitzer, who had given his approval to Hitler's manipulated plebiscite of 1938, did so in the hope of averting an even worse fate for the Austrian Church. He had been pressurized and finally allowed himself to be more or less coerced by a small group of Catholic laymen who believed that by putting 'Heil Hitler!' under his signature he could pave the way for a new and better relationship between the Church and the Nazi regime. The document bearing the six signatures of the men who pressurized the cardinal still exists in our archdiocesan archives in Vienna. Innitzer was not an anti-Semite. He tried to get visas for a large number of Jews who turned to him for help, and repeatedly wrote to Pope Pius XII that he needed money to get Jews out of the country. The answers he received from the Vatican were usually evasive: 'Yes, we will help, but we haven't got the money at the moment', etc. It was not until 1960 that all the material on Innitzer in the archives was sorted. It is now quite clear that hundreds of Viennese Jews owe him their lives.

I was in St Pölten, some 60 or 70 kilometres from Vienna, in 1938, when Innitzer appealed to Austrian Catholics to vote for Hitler. When the news reached us, we were somewhat nonplussed. What did this mean? How was it possible for our cardinal to do such a thing? Some thought Innitzer was possibly trying to obtain a certain protection for the Church, but others were very critical and said he had betrayed it. A few months later, at a special Mass in St Stephen's Cathedral in Vienna, which was attended by thousands of young Catholics, Innitzer appealed to the young not to betray their faith and to remember that Jesus Christ was their Führer. He was enthusiastically cheered outside the cathedral afterwards. Revenge was not long in coming. The very next day the Nazis broke into the bishop's palace and ransacked the entire building. When I became Archbishop of Vienna I had one of the oil paintings which was stabbed several times that day fetched up out of the cellars and hung in the conference hall of the bishop's palace. It is a picture of a crucifix, and the slashes made by those Nazi youths are still clearly visible. I left it as it was and it is still hanging there in memory of those tragic days. Innitzer's secretary at the time, Archbishop Jachym, who later became my vicar-general, told me that they had hidden the cardinal in the attics when the Nazis attacked, and that when he came down after they had left he had given a deep sigh and said, 'Thank God. Now I have been vindicated!' I have read all the material we have in the archives about Innitzer and have concluded that he was perhaps a little naïve politically. He was also very impulsive and decided to act far too quickly without thinking beforehand. And one must not forget that he was a Sudeten German and, like many of his countrymen, inclined to be a German nationalist.

I have often been asked why Pius XII did not do more for the Jews, and why the hierarchy did not speak out more courageously in those terrible years between 1933 and the end of World War II. Fear undeniably played a role. First there was the fear that if the Church spoke out too strongly against Hitler and his helpers, Catholics would suffer reprisals. And then there was the fear of Bolshevism. Many Catholics, including Pope Pius XII, were convinced that the Church had more to fear from Boshevism than from Hitler. They thought that Hitler would defeat the Bolshevists and hoped that then his Third Reich would collapse. Those are two posssible explanations in my eyes as to why the Church did not speak out more strongly against Hitler, but they are only explanations and can in no way excuse the Church's behaviour.

There is no doubt at all in my mind that Pope John XXIII personally sowed the first fragile seeds of Christian–Jewish dialogue. When a group of American Jews came to thank him for deleting those passages in the Good Friday liturgy which could and did lead to repudiation of the Jews, he welcomed them with the words, 'I am Joseph, your brother', underlining how important it was for Christians and Jews to love one another like brothers, and, despite the considerable differences between their faiths, to show this love openly as they shared a common origin.

It was Pope John who initiated the brief Council Declaration on the Church's relationship with Judaism which revolutionized Christian–Jewish dialogue. He was determined to put an end to accusations that the Church was anti-Semitic. As Apostolic Delegate in Turkey in the 1940s, he had experienced the plight of Jews fleeing from Nazi persecution. They had brought him grim news, chiefly from Poland, Slovakia and Romania, and many of them owed him their lives as he helped them to get safely to the Holy Land. After the indescribable horrors of the Holocaust, Pope John felt it was imperative for the Church to signal that it loved the Jews, thus in some small way offsetting the hatred they had experienced with a token of love.

Each Council declaration has its own history, but the history of the brief declaration on the Church's relationship to Judaism is certainly one of the most turbulent. The declaration owes its existence to three people without whose unwavering determination, dedication and patience this briefest of all declarations would never have come about. They were Pope John himself, Cardinal Bea and Prelate Johannes Österreicher, an Austrian priest and convert from Judaism who fled from Austria to the USA at the beginning of World War II. Österreicher was a personal friend of mine. Already as a curate in Vienna in the 1930s, long before other theologians, he concentrated on that theology which Christianity and Judaism had in common. *Nostra Aetate* was the crowning achievement of his life.

Shortly after his election, Pope John asked Cardinal Bea to reflect on how the Jewish question could be incorporated into the Council. I was invited to join this small circle early on and thus experienced at close hand the many crises and continual ups and downs this brief declaration went through. It is indeed a miracle that it was ever passed at all.

Rumours that a pronouncement on the Jewish question was on the Council agenda began circulating almost as soon as the Council opened. With the exception of a small minority of ultra-conservative bishops, the Holocaust preyed on the majority of the Council Fathers' minds and caused us all to re-examine the manifold forms of anti-Semitism which had brought such shame on Europe over the centuries. The mere fact that the question was to be discussed at all, however, immediately met with violent opposition from the Arab world, the Eastern Churches and from the small but vociferous conservative group of Council Fathers around Archbishop Lefebvre. I have the highest admiration for Pope John, Cardinal Bea and Fr Österreicher that they persevered despite fierce opposition, intrigue and downright slander. Right up to the end of the Council this opposition mobilized the mass media and evoked diplomatic protests from the Arab states. I received sacks of letters, many of them from Christians in the Middle East, begging me to prevent a declaration on the Jewish question. Some of the pamphlets that were circulated were positively vicious and libellous. When the small group of Council Fathers that was so against any declaration on the subject saw that they could not prevent it, they tried to water it down and continually lodged complaints so that the drafts had to be changed at least four or five times. Finally, however, on 28 October 1965, *Nostra Aetate* was passed. 2,221 Council Fathers voted in favour, 88 against and three abstained. It had taken four years to reach agreement on this briefest of all the Council declarations.

Before a proper dialogue between Christians and Jews could begin, however, a great deal of debris had to be cleared away – more perhaps than in any other field. The interpretation and exegesis of the New Testament over the centuries, when Christianity was dominant in the world, in no small way contributed towards intensifying anti-Judaistic prejudices. The fact that the mass annihilation of Jews instigated and carried out by the Nazis met with so little resistance shows that a latent feeling of aggression towards Judaism and Jews must already have existed beforehand. It was these prejudices against Jews, indirectly at any rate, that made it possible for a mental attitude to grow which later became a component of anti-Semitism. It was not until the mid-twentieth century that a shift in outlook occurred, triggered no doubt by the horrors of the Holocaust. There is such a thing as the power of evil. It is not rooted in history, however, but grows in people's hearts. If we ask ourselves how such an escalation of evil was possible then we must face the question of personal guilt, for there is no such thing as collective guilt for us to hide behind. Guilt can only be overcome through open admission and a show of remorse.

We have come a long way since Vatican II, thank God. The dialogue between Catholics and Jews has deepened and our relationship has become more mature. The Catholic Church, and especially the present Pope, tirelessly condemn all manifestations of anti-Semitism whenever they crop up. For 30 years now, since 1974, the Vatican commission for religious relations with the Jews has been part of the Pontifical Council for Promoting Christian Unity – which shows that the Church does not consider Judaism and Christianity two completely separate religions, but rather that they are closely linked through the Bible they share. As so often in Christian–Jewish dialogue, the present Pope found the right words in Mainz in 1980 when he said, 'The Old and New Testaments are in dialogue with one another within the Church.'

Human relationships are of crucial importance in overcoming prejudices and bridging rifts. I learnt that at the

Second Vatican Council. The observations made by the large group of non-Catholic observers, with whom the Council Fathers were able to exchange ideas before and after the sessions and which included representatives of Judaism, found their way into many a final document. Dialogue is essential if we are to preserve the ethical values we have in common and be vigilant together so that the terrible mistakes that occurred in the past are never repeated. We must never break this dialogue off.

5

Christian–Muslim dialogue

My interest in Islam as one of the great world religions, and more especially as one of the three monotheistic religions, goes back to my student days in the early 1930s when I studied comparative religion at the Biblical Institute in Rome. It was thanks to Hitler that I was able to continue these studies during World War II, as the Nazis soon forbade the teaching of religion at school, and so I lost my job as an RE teacher in St Pölten where I was cathedral priest at the time. This meant that next to my pastoral duties I was able to enrol at the Oriental Institute of Vienna University and continue with my studies. Vienna is only about 40 miles from St Pölten and I used to go in by train once or twice a week.

My interest in Islam led me to seek the acquaintance of committed Muslims. This became much easier when I became Archbishop of Vienna in 1956, and I was soon in touch with several prominent Muslims. Two years later, on a visit to Beirut, I was able to talk to Muslim leaders and visit their mosques.

Shortly before I left Vienna for Bombay in November 1964 to attend the World Eucharistic Congress with Paul VI, the Egyptian ambassador in Vienna, whom I knew

well, invited me to visit Egypt on my way back from
India. It was an official invitation from the Egyptian government. I accepted, but the invitation worried me. We
were getting towards the end of Vatican II. The third session had just finished and we had at last, in principle at
any rate, been able to reach agreement on *Nostra Aetate*,
the Council Declaration on the Relationship of the
Church to the Non-Christian Religions. (The declaration
was not actually passed until September 1965 during the
last session of the Council.) I had been deeply involved
in the struggle to formulate this declaration over the previous three years. As it dealt with inter-religious dialogue
and above all with the Jewish question, it had met with
fierce opposition from the start and was one of the most
disputed Council declarations. The Council had no
sooner opened in October 1962 when rumours that a
document on the Jewish question was being prepared
began to circulate and met with violent opposition by the
Arab states who argued that the Jewish question was a
political issue. Any pronouncement on it by the Council would politically benefit the state of Israel, and the
Arab states therefore had a duty to oppose it, they
argued. A small but powerful minority of Council
Fathers was also determined to do everything within its
power to stop the declaration going through. Thus the
Preparatory Commission had already wanted to cross it
off the list of Council documents before the Council actually started. It was therefore a small miracle that we had
been able to reach agreement at all. I was naturally somewhat uneasy about visiting an Arab country at this point.
It was just conceivable that prominent Muslims might ask

me to support the Arab cause as far as the Council declaration was concerned.

Before I left Bombay for Cairo, I naturally informed Pope Paul VI of my intention to stop over in Egypt on my way home. We shared a common interest in Islam and were both admirers of the French Orientalist and Islamic scholar Louis Massignon, who did so much to promote Muslim–Christian dialogue. His studies of Islamic mysticism, a little-known chapter of Muslim religious literature, had led him back to the Catholic faith of his childhood. From then on he devoted his life to introducing Christians to the wealth and treasures of Islamic mysticism. He wanted to underline what was permanent in this literature, and therefore also applied to Christians. Massignon never tired of emphasizing the bonds between the three monotheistic religions, and he and his followers are rightly seen as the trailblazers of Christian–Muslim dialogue.

Paul VI understood my reasons for wanting to go to Egypt, but although we discussed my forthcoming visit, the decision to accept the Egyptian government's invitation was entirely my own and I bore the sole responsibility.

On the flight to Cairo I kept thinking of the sacks of protest letters I had received from Arab statesmen asking me to prevent the Council declaration on the Jewish question, and prayed that no attempt would be made to involve me in a political issue. As it turned out, I need not have worried. I was warmly welcomed by the Egyptian government who were delighted to show me their country. I was even able to fulfil a long-standing wish and visit the renowned University of Al Azhar, the oldest and most celebrated of all Islamic academic institutes and the spritual centre of the Islamic world. Only a few years previous to my visit, new faculties of medicine and engineering had been added. Sheikh El Boukary, then Rector of Al Azhar, was genuinely pleased to meet me and show me round, and to my great surprise asked me if I would address his students. I explained that as it was getting close to Christmas, I had to get back to Vienna, but we agreed that I would come back at a later date. 'Is that a promise?' he asked as we parted. I assured him that it was. Back in Vienna I promptly received a call from the Egyptian ambassador asking me to fix a date. We agreed that the following March (1965) would be a good time. That would give me ample time to prepare my address. It was the first time that a Catholic cardinal had been asked to hold an address at Al Azhar and I was more than a little apprehensive as to how well what I had to say on the importance of monotheism, the subject I had chosen to speak on, would go down. On my arrival in Cairo, one of the first questions Sheikh El Boukary asked me was what would I be wearing for the lecture. 'We would consider it a great honour if you came in full regalia and wore a robe of many colours,' he said, and gave me to understand that that would be the best way of showing my respect for Islam and at the same time bearing witness to my own Catholic faith. I had to explain that even on exceptional occasions, Roman Catholic cardinals only ever wore red.

I am calm by temperament and not easily ruffled, but when I saw that sea of Muslim faces looking up at me in the main hall of Al Azhar I could feel my heart pounding. How would they react to what I had to say? What if my views gave offence? My address was entitled 'Monotheism in today's world'. I held it in English, but it was simultaneously translated into Arabic. After tracing the history of monotheism and underlining its persuasiveness, I pointed out how imperative it was, in a world that was rapidly becoming one, for Christianity and Islam, which were not only religions of the Book, but the two most widespread world religions, to respect each other's beliefs and review what they had in common. I was careful to emphasize that the belief that there was no grace outside the Catholic Church had been rejected and that for Christians it was now clear that the grace of God could also be found in non-Christian religions. This was after all March 1965. The Second Vatican Council was not yet over and I thought it improbable that news of the agreement reached on *Nostra Aetate* had reached the Muslim world. I ended my address with an appeal for Muslims and Christians to work together against atheism, agnosticism and indifference. To my relief, my address met with a most positive response and even got favourable headline commentaries, not only in the main Egyptian daily *El Ahram*, but worldwide. From then on I did my best to contact Muslim theologians and religious leaders in the interests of Christian–Muslim dialogue.

In 1968 I was invited by Teheran University to speak on the influence Zarathustra had had on the European and Anglo-Saxon world. It was sometimes also possible to combine visits to Oriental Orthodox Churches with visits to Muslim leaders. When I visited the Syrian

Orthodox Patriarch in Damascus in 1978, for instance, I was also able to talk to the spiritual head of the Syrian Muslims, Grand Mufti Ahmed Kaftaro, who asked me to speak in the Grand Mosque. Like myself, Kaftaro was convinced that the three monotheistic religions, Judaism, Islam and Christianity, must work together for world peace. He was committed to bringing Christianity and Islam closer together after years of conflict and estrangement. I invited him to visit Vienna the following year where he held a notable address at Vienna University on what Christianity and Islam had in common. The time was ripe to put aside the misunderstandings of the past, he said, recalling that the Quor'an held both Jesus and Moses in the highest esteem. 'Whosoever does not believe in Jesus and in the holiness of his teaching is not a Muslim,' he emphasized.

Contacts of this kind grew more difficult over the years and I am not sure whether a Catholic cardinal would be welcome at Al Azhar today, which is sad. Christian–Muslim dialogue has continued, however – as indeed it must in the light of increasing terrorism and fundamentalism. With the increase of Islamic extremism, and particularly since the tragic events of 11 September 2001 and their aftermath, both sides have, however, become noticeably more apprehensive.

There is a broad spectrum of theological persuasions and schools of thought within Islam: from the militant forms, which aim at the complete Islamization of society, to those Muslims who want to draw Islam out of its isolation. One of the biggest differences, and therefore one of the greatest obstacles between Islam and Christianity, is that except in those few Islamic countries like Egypt and Turkey where attempts have been made to introduce laicization, and which I cannot go into here, religious belief and political power are inseparably linked. To use Ayatolla Khomeini's words, 'Without politics Islam is nothing.' Religion and the state are identical. Islamic society, that is the Islamic state, thus has a twofold commitment – a political and a religious commitment. Not only all religious obligations, like prayer, fasting and almsgiving, but also all legal regulations are included in this combination of religion and political power. In how far there is still room for tolerance, freedom of conscience and human rights in a theocracy of this kind is a moot point. I am fully aware that most Muslims will see this differently, but it is nevertheless a question that must be asked. Although freedom of conscience is laid down in the Quor'an, which specifically states that 'there is no compulsion in religion', in practice this is often not the case. Judaism and Christianity as religions of the Book are on the whole shown greater tolerance than other religions, but in a considerable number of Islamic countries, Muslims who convert to Christianity, for instance, still risk their lives in doing so.

One of the reasons why dialogue between Christians and Muslims is difficult, not only at the top, theological level, but even more so at the grass roots, is because Christians and Muslims fear one another. The Crusades were a mortifying experience for the Muslim world. That is why it is certainly not helpful to speak of a 'crusade against terrorism' today. The word has traumatic associations. The sheer force of history which so often

89

resurfaces in conflicts – as, for example, in the recent Balkan War – must never be overlooked. The Crusades, and later colonialism, but also the present scientific and technological supremacy of the Western world, on which so many Muslim countries have come to depend, have made Muslims feel deeply inferior. Muslim students who study at Western universities, moreover, often take back liberal and enlightened ideas with them which influence intellectual circles in their home countries and are seen as a threat to Islamic society. All this has only served to fan the flames of anti-Western feeling and led to a positive reappraisal of those forces in Islam which consolidate the orderliness of society and 'prove' how much better it is than the decadent, amoral and 'godless' West.

Many people in the West, including many Christians, are also frightened of Muslims. The idea that religion and the state are one and that religion should dominate the entire state apparatus is inconceivable and unacceptable for people who believe in democracy. Reports that in some Islamic countries Christians are considered second-class citizens, or even risk persecution, and that Islamic extremists plan a 'jihad' or holy war against the West make Christians deeply uneasy. And when Muslims who live in the West utter fanatic anti-Western diatribes that do not exactly suggest a willingness for dialogue, this uneasiness increases and often turns to resentment and anger.

One of the root causes of fear is ignorance, and the best remedy for ignorance is knowledge; in this case getting to know more about each other's religions and improving the basis for dialogue.

According to specialists on the subject, the large majority of Muslims outside Europe still think that Christian–Muslim dialogue is permissible and therefore possible, but that it is superfluous as Islam is the final and perfect form of religion. At the top level, however, in the Muslim World Congress, Muslims are becoming increasingly aware that in a world that is fast becoming one, Muslims and Christians must learn to live with one another. This will only be possible if they respect one another, try to avoid misunderstandings and learn to solve conflicts without violence. I hope that the as yet small group of Muslims who are in favour of honest dialogue will grow and that we will all learn to differentiate between Muslims who are genuinely filled with hatred and those who reject hatred as much as we do. The Second Vatican Council specifically stresses that the Catholic Church holds Muslims in high regard and urges Christians and Muslims to forget the past and make a sincere effort 'to achieve mutual understanding for the benefit of all'.

As fundamentalism is on the rise worldwide, it is essential to understand how fundamentalists think, as we will have to learn to live with them. Not everyone who is branded a fundamentalist really is one. In his book *The Revenge of God*, the French sociologist Gilles Kepel shows that a renaissance of the monotheistic religions is only apparently linked with fundamentalism. It would be wrong to accuse all the members of strict religious movements of being fundamentalists. Nor is every fervent profession of faith fundamentalist unless it is combined with aggressive behaviour towards others.

I would differentiate between the fundamentalism which emerged in North America at the end of the nineteenth century and European fundamentalism which has a slightly different background and associations. North American fundamentalism was a reaction against liberal theology, modern Bible exegesis and modern science. To counter these new developments, fundamentalists in North America emphasized the need to defend the Bible and the principles on which the Christian faith is based. They believe in the literal and absolute inerrancy of the scriptures.

European fundamentalism is related to but not identical with the US form. Unlike Protestant fundamentalism in the USA, the European form has a pejorative connotation. You will hear many people speak of fundamentalism in Europe, but no one likes to be called a fundamentalist. It is not a case of defending the Bible but of opposing the modern, secularized world against which fundamentalists want to defend themselves and their faith. This means resisting religious pluralism, religious freedom and freedom of conscience, as in fundamentalist eyes these are the very things things that endanger the principles of a fundamentalist's faith. After the Second Vatican Council, for example, concern for the Catholic Church's irreversible Christian heritage, which a small but tenacious minority thought endangered, grew. Until he was excommunicated, Lefebvre was the standard-bearer of an aggressive, fundamentalist, innerchurch campaign against ecumemism, religious freedom and all liberal and democratic tendencies in the Church. Sentences from Vatican II declarations were taken out of context and used to increase people's uncertainty and mistrust of the so-called 'others'.

Fundamentalist tendencies join forces across all religious and cultural borders. Fair discussions in written or spoken form often become impossible. 'Other people's' arguments or answers are not welcome. Fundamentalists believe that the endangered foundation of their faith can only be rescued by 'true believers' who cling to the past and to tradition. This leads to mistrust, bitterness and denunciation, all of which are on the increase at the moment. Clashes become more frequent and solidarity is weakened. Whenever fanatics utilize any of the world's religions, the outcome is appalling. If for political reasons God is drawn into political conflicts as an ally, the result has always been an explosive brew.

The growing presence of Islam in Europe has made Europeans more apprehensive of Islam. When certain leading Muslims say that where the modern Western world gains a foothold, people lose their identity, their culture, their values and norms, this heightens fundamentalist trends in the West.

While fundamentalism should not be overestimated and suspected round every corner, as that only makes the general climate in society worse, it must not be underestimated and treated it as if it were just a passing vogue, either. Fundamentalists cannot be 'converted' in round-table talks and even less in TV discussions. On the contrary, debates of this kind are always counterproductive and achieve exactly the opposite. The most important thing is to get to know a fundamentalist's bogeyman. The way in which a fundamentalist views the world is reflected in this bogeyman. During the Cold War, communism was the bogeyman in the USA. In Europe at the moment it is our modern, secularized world with its religious liberalism or subjectivism. The more complicated the political and economic situation of the world becomes, the more people fall for charismatic, at times even 'charis-manic', personalities who tend to oversimplify and therefore mislead. The result is a black-and-white picture of the world which refuses to recognize the fact that we live in a multicultural society.

The only way forward is through personal dialogue, setting an example that instils trust and is based on one's own clear, religious principles. It is our only chance of untwisting minds and of gently leading the conversation round to a more critical view of a fundamentalist's hate figure and finding the lowest common denominator as a basis for further dialogue. It is essential to avoid making fundamentalists uncertain as that would render the dialogue futile. One must also always bear in mind that one cannot force anyone to indulge in dialogue.

6

Inter-religious dialogue

Already at a very early age I wondered what it was like to speak a different language or have a different faith. Foreign words on tins or cardboard boxes immediately attracted my attention. Soon after that I must have become aware of the fact that there were people out there in the world who spoke a different language from mine and had a different faith from my own. Both discoveries intrigued me as I was surrounded by people who all spoke the same language and all shared the same faith. How, I wondered, did these people who spoke different languages and had different religions get on with one another? This early fascination for languages and world religions was probably providential, as it not only remained with me throughout my life, but languages and the study of comparative religion became two of my main – and favourite – occupations. It was therefore only natural, I suppose, that Christianity's relationship to other religions later became one of my foremost interests.

I have spent many years of my life thinking about this most significant issue, and the study of comparative religions has become a second way to Christ; but of course, I too went through a period of great uncertainty.

Was my faith the same as other faiths? Were there differences – and if so, why?

For centuries Christianity claimed that it was superior to other religions. Europeans took Christianity out into the world, to the European colonies, and arrogantly claimed that theirs was the 'only true religion'. That, tragically, was a mistaken belief in Western supremacy. The backlash came when certain modern scholars of comparative religion declared all religions equal. My own conclusion lies somewhere in the middle. As a Christian I believe that God spoke to us through Jesus Christ, but for that very reason I am bound to marvel at and respect the wealth and profusion we find in other religions. We have a privileged position as Christians, but we must be humble and understand that Christ's message goes beyond us. We must go on striving to understand what God's plans are for the different religions. I have no difficulty in recognizing that other religions are also seeking to find the truth. Some Catholics think that those who indulge in religious dialogue, who are prepared in all honesty to discuss their beliefs with non-Christians at eye level, so to speak, while making no attempt to 'convert' them, are in danger of losing their faith and moreover betraying their own faith. Actually, just the opposite is the case. The more involved I become in inter-religious dialogue, the deeper my own convictions become.

Unlike in mathematics, religious beliefs cannot be proved. There are excellent reasons for believing, but in the final instance, faith remains a personal decision. That is why one can never force anyone to believe. So it is not a question of laying claim to the truth, or proving which religion is superior. Dialogue means respecting others as human beings, even if in the end the partners beg to differ. The only way we can avoid war and conflict is through inter-religious dialogue of this kind, and it is crucial that we keep this dialogue open and go on encouraging it despite alarmist warnings or fundamentalist opposition.

The four cardinal virtues are all-important here: prudence – which enables one to judge the consequences of one's own actions; justice – as the principle to give to each his own; fortitude – as the courage to bear witness; and temperance as self-discipline and finding the golden mean. To these we should nowadays perhaps add four more as they are decisive for ethical behaviour in today's world: tolerance, respect, solidarity and love of peace. Tolerance is decisive if we are to live together in peace in a multicultural society. It is not only a concept, but an element of human behaviour which can be acquired through special training. But it must be the right kind of tolerance. We must distinguish between formal tolerance and real tolerance. Formal tolerance automatically accepts different points of view without question and often springs from indifference. It is negative: prejudices and contradictions remain and can result in arrogance and ostracism. Real tolerance, on the other hand, means freely recognizing that opinions can differ and attempting to learn from one another so that prejudices can be put aside and respect for the opinion of others can grow. Love of peace, in its turn, is decisive for international understanding. And solidarity is the conviction that we are 'all in one boat'.

Vatican II completely changed the Church's attitude to other religions. It was the first time that a Council specifically pointed to the value of other religions.

People look to their different religions for an answer to the unsolved riddles of human existence. The problems that weigh heavily on people's hearts are the same today as in past ages. What is the meaning and purpose of life? What is upright behaviour, and what is sinful? Where does suffering originate and what end does it serve? How can genuine happiness be found? What happens at death? What is judgement? What reward follows death? And finally, what is that ultimate mystery, beyond human explanation, which embraces our entire existence, from which we take our origin and toward which we tend? (*Nostra Aetate*, 1)

The Catholic Church rejects nothing of what is true and holy in these religions . . . Yet it proclaims and is in duty bound to proclaim without fail, Christ who is the way, the truth and the life. (*Nostra Aetate*, 2)

Nostra Aetate explains that in a world in which people are drawing closer together, the Church 'is examining its relations with the non-Christian religions more carefully'. It is important to note here that the Council does not ask whether there are such 'relations', but 'what kind of relations' exist, and it says that these must be encouraged. The question is significant, the decree explains, because it is the Church's duty to foster 'unity and charity among nations'.

It was while *Nostra Aetate* was being written in December 1964 that I accompanied Pope Paul VI to the World Eucharistic Congress in Bombay. After emphasizing that India was a country of ancient cultures and the cradle of great religions, Pope Paul quoted the following passage from the *Upanishads*, 'From the unreal lead me to the real. From darkness lead me to light. From death lead me to immortality.' And on another occasion Paul VI said, 'We must get closer to one another, not only with the help of modern means of communication or through the media, but through the heart.' His words made a deep impression in India at the time. It was then that I was asked to invite representatives of the main religions to a 'talk on religion' – a first in those days. No mention yet of the word 'dialogue'. We sat at a kind of elevated round table in a packed hall – I think there were four or five speakers, a Muslim, a Hindu, a Buddhist, a Parsee and myself – and each of us got up in turn and explained the essential aspects of his religion. It was all very formal. There was no discussion and of course no outcome, but it was a first cautious 'sending out of feelers', and in the light of what had gone before, a significant signal of change.

Only quite recently I received a small package from India. On opening it, I found the memoirs of Fr Joseph Neuner, an Austrian Jesuit who has spent most of his life in India. He was a *peritus* (adviser) at the Second Vatican Council whose experience in India and knowledge of Hinduism were invaluable when the text on the Church's attitude towards non-Christian religions was being drafted. I was glad to read in his memoirs how great an impact the Council had had on his later work in India which has chiefly been concerned with the formation of Indian priests. I had to smile when I looked at his portrait on the cover. His face, which is so familiar to me as we have known each other for years, seems somehow to have taken on an Indian look, and although I may well be imagining things, to me there is something very Indian about his smile and the look in his eyes. Is that perhaps not a sign that inculturation has worked?

One spectacular outcome of the Council was the World Day of Prayer for Peace in Assissi in 1986. Pope John Paul II had invited the representatives of the world religions to come to Assissi to pray for peace. Although they did not all join in common prayer together, but each prayed separately, certain over-anxious or oppositional circles immediately accused the Pope of being caught up in the maelstrom of modern relativism. They were wrong. Assissi first of all sent out a strong signal that the Catholic Church was committed to the promotion of peace and solidarity in the world. And second, the Assissi meeting almost wordlessly disposed of numerous scholarly treatises, comments and disputes that had been published in the science of comparative religion in the second half of the nineteenth and first half of the twentieth centuries, and put the prime focus on the strength and effective force of religion for the future of humankind.

Today, inter-religious dialogue is crucial in our

pluralistic global culture. Whereas formerly Christians knew very little about other civilizations and saw members of non-Christian religions as 'heathens' or 'idolators' and their religions as superstitions or false religions, inter-religious dialogue has opened up new insights.

Over the past decades, a considerable number of religious historians have turned their attention to the study of the great religions, and to the issue of religious pluralism, which is of such significance today as the world is fast becoming one in so many ways through the process of globalization. The pioneers proceeded predominantly from a Western standpoint, with Western concepts of cultural and religious history, and from the viewpoint of the Western Enlightenment and Western secularization. Now, however, this virgin theological ground is beginning to interest Christians in other parts of the world, especially in Asia.

Fr Jacques Dupuis SJ has emerged as the most important thinker on the issue of how Christianity should understand itself in a world where other religions can no longer be ignored or taken for granted. He spent almost 40 years in India and more than twenty of those 40 years teaching theology at an interational theological college near Darjeeling where he was able to engage in dialogue with representatives from many of the great religious traditions of the world – Buddhists, Christians, Confucianists and Hindus. He then returned to Rome and taught Christology at the Gregorian – my own university – until he retired. His experience and knowledge of other religious traditions, together with his specialized knowledge of Jesus Christ, make him eminently qualified and ideally suited in every way to be a leading Christian representative in inter-religious dialogue.

I can still remember my excitement on receiving his masterly work *Toward a Christian Theology of Religious Pluralism* in 1997. I found it fascinating and studied it intently for days. It was followed in 2001 by *Christianity and the Religions* which is also excellent. I was touched to see that it was dedicated to me. Dupuis courageously explores the fundamental question of precisely how God's saving presence is mediated to those who practise non-Christian religions. He suggests that the most likely means is through their religious traditions. But he is quick to emphasize that this does not mean that he regards other religions as equal partners with Christianity in God's plan of salvation. Whatever value they possess, they owe to their 'participation' in the saving work of the one and unique mediator, Jesus Christ. Dupuis makes it clear that he has been encouraged in his explorations by what Pope John Paul II has written on this subject, and quotes him frequently. He realizes he is exploring new ground, but says 'a qualitative leap' on the part of the Church is expedient if we are to acquire a new respect for other world religions. I agree with him wholeheartedly. That is why I defended him against the accusations made against him by the Congregation for the Doctrine of the Faith in 1998 – accusations which were luckily later resolved. I was very glad to see that when the Gregorian celebrated its 450th anniversary in 2001, the Pope acknowledged Fr Dupuis's 'pioneering' work on the meaning of the different religions in God's plan for the salvation of mankind.

Inter-religious Dialogue

When I was young, I was only able to read about other religions in books. Now our ecumenical and inter-faith dialogue partners live among us as neighbours and colleagues. We must ask ourselves what it means to be a Catholic today among so many other religions. This is no doubt one of the most important questions of the millennium – a very difficult question, which many will need help with. We know that revelation is finished but important questions remain. Have we understood everything that has been revealed? Might new personal insights not be possible in the future? What do we mean when we say that revelation is finished? Would it not be possible for certain events to occur which would give us, not new revelation – the answer of the Church is clear on that – but a new interpretation of revelation?

That is probably what those engaged in building bridges between Christianity and the other great world religions feel. All these religions seek answers to those ultimate human questions – where do we come from, where are we going and what is the meaning of our lives? If I believe in the activity of the Holy Spirit the world over, maybe there are new insights – not revelations – to come. Do we as Westerners really know enough about a non-Western mentality as in Asia, for instance? Only dialogue will help us to gain new insights in this field.

7

Dialogue with non-believers

Although small and not in the limelight at the time, the three secretariats that were set up during the Second Vatican Council were to play a crucial role in opening the Church's doors to the world. I have already discussed the Secretariats for the Promotion of Christian Unity and Inter-religious Dialogue and come now to the third secretariat, which was first known as the Secretariat for Non-Believers.

In February 1965, after the third session of the Council, Pope Paul VI came up to me and asked me to head a third secretariat that would seek dialogue with all people of goodwill who were looking for answers but who were neither Christians nor members of other religions, a secretariat that would engage in dialogue with so-called 'non-believers'. I must admit that I was a little taken aback. 'If you had asked me to take over the Secretariat for Inter-Religious Dialogue, a subject with which I'm fairly familiar, I would have had some ideas on how to proceed, but dialogue with non-believers, with atheists? I am somewhat nonplussed . . . How do I even begin?' '*Usus docebit*,' the Pope said calmly, which more or less means 'Just start and you'll learn as you go along.'

Dialogue with Non-Believers

Nowadays one would probably say 'learning by doing'. I agreed, but on condition that I could remain in Vienna and not have to move to Rome.

The Secretariat for Non-Believers was founded two months later, in April 1965. The beginnings were certainly not easy. We were given a small office in Trastevere. Karl Rahner and the fundamental theologian Johann Baptist Metz were two of the first members. That summer, before the final session of the Council, we were invited to a conference in Salzburg on 'Human Beings and their Religion' organized by the 'Paulus-Gesellschaft', a free association of Catholic academics, above all from the Federal Republic of Germany, who were trying to bring leading Marxists, scientists who were Christians and theologians together. Unfortunately several communist intellectuals were refused visas by their own governments and so could not attend. After the conference was over, both the Marxists and the Christians had to admit that they were not at all familiar with each other's views.

The declaration on atheism had not yet been passed by the Council. It was a very controversial issue and, at the beginning of the fourth and final session in September 1965, led to one of the most heated debates at the Council. The majority of the Council Fathers were against declaring atheism anathema, but a minority wanted it condemned. Cardinal Franjo Seper of Zagreb, the Melkite Catholic patriarch, Maximus IV Sayegh, and I were of the opinion that Christians were partly to blame for the increase in secularization. I also stressed that militant atheism was only one form of atheism and that it was imperative to differentiate between the different

105

forms. We should first investigate the different forms that existed worldwide and find out what caused them, and then discuss possible means of combating atheism together with the other Christian Churches. Banning atheism was not in the spirit of the Council. No one should be declared anathema, I emphasized. The reason why we did not expressly mention communism by name was because Vatican II avoided any mention of countries or forms of government in the Council declarations.

The eighth and final version of *Gaudium et Spes*, The Pastoral Constitution on the Church in the Modern World in which atheism is discussed, was finally passed in December 1965. 2,309 bishops voted against banning atheism, 75 were in favour of declaring it anathema and seven votes were invalid. Joseph Ratzinger, then a young theologian, said it was most positive that the Church had neither expressly mentioned communism nor condemned it, and the fact that it had decided to take this step was a milestone in twentieth-century church history.

The Secretariat for Non-Believers was based on Pope John's appeal to the Church to open its doors to all people of goodwill and on Paul VI's encyclical *Ecclesiam Suam* which stressed the importance of dialogue with the whole world. They were, so to speak, the new secretariat's charter. In *Ecclesiam Suam* Pope Paul had likened the three secretariats to three concentric circles. The first and largest circle encompassed the entire human race. This vast circle included many people who professed no religion at all. From now on they were 'my' secretariat's concern. The second, smaller circle comprised the non-Christian religions, and the third and smallest circle embraced the separated Christian Churches.

During the last session of the Council, Paul VI made 23 bishops from different countries, including bishops from communist countries in Eastern Europe, members of the Secretariat for Non-Believers.

One of the secretariat's immediate aims was to promote the study of the three main forms of atheism, that is Marxist atheism based on dialectical materialism, humanist atheism based on technical and economic progress, and agnostic atheism which manifested itself as indifference to religion and had nothing to do with either of the former two. The secretariat did not deal with communism as a political form, or with relations between the Church and countries under communist rule. It had nothing to do with communist leaders who visited the Pope, for instance. In 1968 it was expanded. One of the new members was the then auxiliary bishop of São Paolo, Paulo Evaristo Arns.

Once again my primary concern was a pastoral one. At a press conference in Vienna I stressed how important ecumenical co-operation was in combating increasing secularism, and that it was imperative to define terms such as secularization and pluralism more precisely as they were so often loosely used by the media. Many of us were never really happy with the term 'non-believers': it sounded so negative. It was suggested that 'Secretariat for Dialogue with Today's World' or 'Secretariat for Dialogue with the Secular World' would be more appropriate, but the General Assembly decided against changing the name.

We soon saw that the central office in Rome could not manage alone and that national, regional and local secretariats were essential. All bishops' conferences were therefore asked to set up secretariats for non-believers which would study secularization and go into the possibilities of dialogue.

In March 1969 the University of California, Berkeley and the Agnelli Foundation organized a conference on the 'Culture of Non-Belief' in Rome. One of the participants was the Czech philosopher Milan Machovec who explained that many Marxists were already against what he called 'brutal Marxism' and believed in an atheism committed to dialogue. Machovec was a supporter of Alexander Dubcek and in favour of 'communism with a human face'. When Soviet tanks rolled through Prague in August 1968 and crushed the 'Prague Spring', Machovec was in Austria. He declined all invitations to stay. 'One cannot first be in favour of giving socialism based on Marxist theory "a human face", and then, when those who call themselves communists show their grotesque faces, flee abroad. I belong in Prague.' So he returned, but of course immediately lost his job as a university professor. He managed to keep himself and his family alive by giving private lessons and doing odd jobs like playing the organ at a Catholic church. It was at this time that he wrote his famous book *Jesus for Atheists* which has been translated into fifteen languages. He also wrote a book on Pope John XXIII whom he always said he 'loved like a son' because he did not only speak about love but 'really loved us all . . . Buddhists, Protestants and atheists'. His knowledge of the Bible was quite remarkable for a so-called 'non-believer' (which only goes to show how inappropriate the word is), and he was in contact with many famous theologians like Karl Barth, Karl Rahner and Jürgen Moltmann.

The French Jesuit theologian Jean Daniélou, who had meanwhile become a member of the secretariat, the Baptist theologian H. Cox and the American sociologist Peter Berger also took part in that conference. Daniélou was made a cardinal a month later at the consistory in April 1969.

In July 1969 the secretariat organized a regional conference in Tokyo on 'Secularism and Atheism' and invited Buddhist and Hindu observers. Up to then we had approached the project with European eyes but it immediately became clear that Western concepts and views did not apply in Asia. Non-belief or unbelief, secularism and indifference not only varied from continent to continent, but from region to region.

We reached much the same conclusions in Mexico that September. The situation there was perhaps similar to that in Europe, but for the Latin American representatives secularization and atheism were seen as liberation from oppression.

In 1972, two conferences were organized simultaneously in Africa, one in Abidjan for the French-speaking countries, and one in Kampala for the English-speaking countries. I attended the one in Kampala. We discovered that there were very few non-believers in Africa, at least not yet at the time. The few that there were had studied abroad at Western universities, but secularism and indifference to religion were on the increase. With the help of the local bishops' conferences, it was decided to establish one secretariat for non-believers in the English-speaking countries in Africa and one for the French-speaking countries.

In June 1974 I decided to visit Yugoslavia – a country which seemed to be going its own way. I wanted to see if an opening for dialogue with non-believers was perhaps possible. Tito had after all expressed appreciation of the Church's and the Pope's efforts for peace, of aid to developing countries and even of ecumenism, and I was determined to try to engage in dialogue. Although as usual my visit was not official, this was the only one of my visits to Eastern Europe on which I talked to government officials.

When I contacted Belgrade, Ljubljana and Zagreb, I was told that as long as the Church did not get involved in politics I was welcome to come and talk. In Ljubljana I met Edvard Kardelj, a close friend of Tito, who was also his ideologist. He personally confirmed what I had been told, namely that as long as I kept off politics, I could discuss whatever I wanted. But I wanted to be quite sure what exactly this meant. 'Say I were to go to one of your secondary schools here and give a lesson in social science. After explaining the Marxist concept, would I be allowed to tell the pupils that Marxism was not the only concept, that other concepts existed and then go on to talk about those other concepts?' His eyebrows rose and, after pausing for a moment, he said, 'In that case it might be better if you were to teach Maths.' 'Fine,' I replied. 'That at least is a clear answer. Now I know where I am.' The signal was obvious. So far and no further.

In the late 1970s, 'Nova Spes', an international, privately funded foundation, that had been set up to study such topics as the relationship between science and religion, invited Nobel Prize winners to a number of conferences in Rome on the ethical and philosophical aspects of environmental problems. I chaired these conferences and especially enjoyed meeting scientists who were interested in religion. Scientists' views on the origin of the universe and, of course, on religion, have always fascinated me and I still regularly discuss the latest developments in science and medicine – insofar as I am capable of following them – with scientists I know in Vienna. I think it was the former editor of *The Tablet*, John Wilkins, who once accused me of wanting to know how God's computer worked. He was right. At one such conference I met the English physicist Sir Nevill Mott, who had only recently received the Nobel Prize for physics. We sat next to one another at lunch. He told me that he had not been brought up in any religion and never went to church as a child, but his wife had become an Anglican and, late in life, he too became a Christian. We talked at length about the Sermon on the Mount, the beauty of the King James version of the Bible and, perhaps naturally, as the Nobel Prize winners had spent some time with Pope John Paul II in private audience that morning, about papal primacy. I still remember the charming way in which he begged to disagree with me on the question of authority! I later read and greatly enjoyed the collection of thought-provoking essays he edited entitled *Can Scientists Believe?* And of course we both immensely enjoyed *The Tablet.*

Meanwhile the then Prefect of the Congregation for the Doctrine of the Faith, Cardinal Franjo Seper, had asked me to engage in dialogue with Austrian Freemasons. Under former canon law, Catholics who became Free-masons were considered in a state of grave sin and excommunicated. I had often discussed the problem with Pope Paul VI and with Cardinal Seper. It seemed that opinion in the Church on Freemasonry differed greatly from country to country. In February 1968, therefore, Cardinal Seper sent bishops' conferences all over the world a number of questions concerning Freemasony. The answers he got were mostly positive. With the exception of Spain, all the European bishops' conferences were in favour of revising the Church's stance on Freemasonry and most were in favour of dialogue with Freemasons. The then president of the English bishops' conference and Archbishop of Westminster, Cardinal John Heenan, said, 'It is my personal opinion that there is no reason-able ground to prevent an English Catholic from becom-ing a Freemason.' And even the Italian bishops' conference wrote that 'Italy, too, should seek opportu-nities for dialogue, and excommunication should be reconsidered.' The new code of canon law, which became valid on 27 November 1983, no longer mentions Freemasons but says that Catholics are forbidden to become members of societies that plot against the Church. The day before the new codex became valid, the Congregation for the Doctrine of the Faith, whose Prefect by then was Cardinal Joseph Ratzinger, issued a decree which said that membership of the Freemasons remained forbidden for Catholics, and violations of this prohibition were gravely sinful. The question of whether or not Catholics who become Freemasons are excommunicated remains disputed to this present day. I raised the matter with Cardinal Ratzinger personally and we wrote to each other and spoke on the subject for over fifteen years. My dialogue with Austrian Freemasons, which was most positive, continued for over 29 years. Since Vatican II the Church has been intent on dialogue with the whole world. What right has it to refuse to dialogue with the World Organization of Freemasons? Dialogue, in whatever form, demands mutual respect and a corresponding willingness to talk to one another. Why should that not be possible with Freemasons?

In 1979 I was approached by the Chinese ambassador in Vienna who told me that China was interested in the Catholic Church's stance on Europe, at that time still divided by the Iron Curtain, and in Pope John Paul II who had only recently been elected. We had several lengthy talks and it was obvious that he was more interested in politics than in religion. One day he asked me if I would be interested in visiting China and talking to Chinese people on a subject of my own choosing. I decided to accept his invitation in the hope that I would be able to find out more about the Chinese government's attitude towards religion and the situation of the religious minorities in China. It was then three years since the end of the Cultural Revolution during which all forms of religious life had been suppressed. I therefore asked the ambassador if it would be all right if I talked on 'The

Future of Religion'. Perfectly all right, he answered. I of course informed Pope John Paul II of my intentions, but again emphasize that the decision to accept the invitation was entirely my own and I had no mandate from the Vatican.

I left Vienna on 9 March 1980. When I arrived in Peking I was met at the airport by representatives of the Chinese People's Association for Friendship with Foreign Countries and driven to my hotel. The next morning I was given a detailed programme of all the events my hosts had planned for my ten-day stay, which included a visit to the Great Wall and to the Chinese opera.

In my address on 'The Future of Religion' I talked openly about my travels to communist countries in Eastern Europe and the experiences I had gathered there, and said that I thought that the outlook for religion in our modern world was definitely positive. I was asked several questions afterwards, mostly about the Vatican's *Ostpolitik* and the situation of the Catholic Church in South America, but also theological questions concerning Europe.

I was able to visit the leaders of the Buddhist and Muslim communities and also the Association of Protestant Christians in China. It seemed that since the overthrow of the Gang of Four and the end of the Cultural Revolution in 1976 it had become easier to practise religion and I was told that religious liberty was 'assured' by the new government.

It was possible for me to talk to two bishops of the Chinese Patriotic Church – Bishop Fu of Peking, who had only recently been ordained, and Bishop Yang, the

General Secretary of the Patriotic Church. We met several times and were able to talk at length. We conversed in Latin, which they spoke fluently, and my impression was that they were both truly Catholic and committed to the Church. Although the Chinese Patriotic Catholic Church is officially a schismatic Church, I could not detect anything schismatic in these bishops' way of thinking. When I asked them if it would be possible for them to visit Austria, however, their answer was evasive. They were not able to give me any figures on how many bishops or priests there were in China and what percentage of the population was Catholic. Mass was still celebrated in the old Tridentine rite in Latin when I was there, but I believe that that has changed now. With financial help from the Austrian Church, all Vatican II documents have since been translated into Chinese. I was not allowed to celebrate Mass myself. I was told that for a long time no one in China had even been told about the Second Vatican Council.

It proved exceedingly difficult to find out anything about the so-called 'Catacomb Church' which has remained loyal to Rome. I would very much have liked to meet some of its members, but unfortunately this was not possible.

My discussions with the director of the Religious Affairs Bureau, Mr Xiao Xianfa, were interesting. He told me that the main reason why the government only recognized the Patriotic Catholic Church, which is state controlled, was because China had had unpleasant experiences of foreign missions and colonialism and therefore rejected any dependence on foreign countries.

That was why no Church in China could be in union with Rome. Mr Xiao knew of the existence of the 'Catacomb Church'. Several of its bishops were in prison, he said, but that was 'for political reasons'. My general impression was that he was quite prepared to be open about the situation.

I headed the Secretariat for Non-Believers, now known as the Pontifical Council for Culture, for fifteen years. I still believe in the power of dialogue and am convinced that the truth will be stronger than all efforts to manipulate it. But above all, I believe that leading a Christian life and setting a Christian example is more powerful than words can ever be. When dialogue proves impossible and all words fail, only one word remains, and that word is love.

8

The all-important
dialogue with God

My parents were good traditional Catholics, as was usual
among country people in Lower Austria before World War
I. We children were of course taught to say our daily
prayers from a very early age and the whole family
attended Mass on Sundays, but I was never an altar boy
or in any way involved in the local parish, and my parents never encouraged me to become a priest. One very
early childhood memory has remained with me all my
life. I was standing or kneeling at the bedside of a dying
relative whom the whole family were accompanying on
the final stretch of his journey. Although I can hardly
have been more than four or five years old, I can still feel
the peace and serenity at that bedside and how I was able
to watch a human being die peacefully, surrounded by
his relatives, and return to the God who made him.

At primary school, however, Religious Instruction, or
Doctrine as it was called then, seemed to me to consist
of a never-ending list of things one was forbidden to do.
I remember trying hard not to sin against the com-
mandments and being very frightened of my first
Confession.

Doctrine did not play a very important role at my

boarding school, the Benedictine Abbey at Melk, either. We had only two periods of the subject a week and the Father who took us for it was very old and frail. I'm afraid I found his lessons rather boring. The atmosphere at Melk Abbey as a whole, however, was surprisingly open-minded for a Catholic school in the 1920s and some of my teachers were wonderful priests. I loved Greek and Latin from the start and was fascinated by classical literature and Greek and Roman history, but I also loved English and French, which I took as voluntary subjects. One of the tasks for our finals was to write a paper on a special subject. I decided to write my paper in Latin and chose 'Women in the Age of Homer' as my subject. It was for this essay that I was offered a choice of two scholarships, one to London and the other to Rome. I chose Rome, perhaps because of my love for the history of the Roman Empire, although the thought of becoming a priest may have been somewhere in the back of my mind. I often think, however, that if I had chosen London I might not have become a priest.

My scholarship was to the Gregorian, the Jesuit university in Rome founded by St Ignatius of Loyola. We alumni from Austria lived at the German College, and in those days (1927) still wore red cassocks, which is why in Rome we were known as *gamberi cotti* ('boiled crabs').

Two events in particular impressed me deeply in those first days in the Eternal City. As Roman history and literature had so fascinated me at school, it was only natural that one of my first outings was to the *Capitol* from where one can to look down onto the *Forum*

Romanum. I still remember how shocked I was to see that all that was left of the once so glorious Roman Empire was just an expanse of ruins. The little that was left seemed to underline all the more forcefully that everything great and wonderful in this world is only transient. The other event that left a deep impression on me was my first Mass at St Peter's. Coming as I did from a small country parish, I was spellbound by the many different faces around me, people from all parts of the world murmuring in different languages as they waited for the Pope to arrive. And then the sudden hush as Pius XI was carried into the Basilica and the flourish of trumpets, followed by Solemn High Mass. What compelling power was capable of bringing together and uniting such diversity, I remember asking myself. Two things about the Church struck me particularly, and for the first time, on that visit to St Peter's – its universality and the dynamism of its spiritual power. I did not realize until much later that those first impressions, the impermanence of all earthly achievements on the one hand, and the spiritual power of Christianity on the other, had a considerable influence on my decision to become a priest.

After studying philosophy for a year, I felt inwardly torn, dissatisfied and overcome by doubt. I don't know where I got the idea, but I took out a copy of Aristotle's *Metaphysics* in Greek and Aquinas's commentary of it. Two different worlds – two different people. With a certain doggedness I studied one chapter of the Aristotle and the corresponding commentary by Aquinas first thing each morning. I remember keeping this up all through my second year until about Easter when I came to the final chapter where Aristotle reaches his conclusion. For him one prime, unmoving originator is the final explanation – to which Aquinas simply adds, 'And that is God *in saecula saeculorum.*' And thus, through the addition of a set liturgical phrase, Aristotle's final conclusion undergoes a Christian transformation. As I was thinking all this through, I heard the Easter bells ringing somewhere in the vicinity. To this day I have never forgotten how a deep inner enlightenment – an inner satisfaction and an immense joy – had grown gradually as my study of the two books progressed, and how these were suddenly echoed in the chimes of those Easter bells.

But it was probably John Henry Newman who had the greatest formative influence on me. I felt, and indeed still feel, a deep spiritual affinity with Newman. I was profoundly impressed by the way he lived and experienced his faith and by his love for truth and honesty. I admired above all his intuitive grasp of religious truths and his psychological insights.

It was at this time that I decided to study comparative religion at the Bible Institute. It was, like so many of the decisions I have made in my life that have later proved providential, an instinctive, spontaneous decision, and one which was considered most unusual for a seminarian at the time. This was in the late 1920s, and not a few eyebrows were raised when I said I wanted to study old oriental languages so that I could read the religious books of the other great world religions in the original, but I was given permission.

I was eager to find out what other religions had to say on such fundamental questions as the meaning of life, on death and on what comes after death in order to base my own arguments on facts. Were all religions equally true or equally false? What difference was there between Jesus Christ and the founders of the other great world religions?

My own religious experiences and the study of other cultures and religions led me to a new and deeper knowledge of the Gospel message. When they set out on their search for the meaning of human life, the founders of the other great world religions proceeded from the human being, whereas Christ says, 'I am the living bread which has come down from heaven' (John 6.51). This was one of the reasons why he and his message were not understood. 'He was in the world that had come into being through him, and the world did not recognize him' (John 1.10). The Christian religion did not spring from the longing of human hearts, nor from historical or sociological laws, but from a mission born of a triune God. Christ's message transcends all other dimensions. It does not only concern the Christian community but the whole of humanity. And his main message was, 'You must love the Lord your God with all you heart, with all your soul and with all your strength, and your neighbour as yourself' (Luke 10.27). This love as an absolute value is the reason why I decided to live Christianity and became a priest. I have never looked back.

There was a time when I wanted to become a Jesuit as I was very much attracted by the high academic standards that were demanded of the members of that order, but the then director of the German College, himself a Jesuit, reminded me that St Ignatius had founded the

German College to train diocesan priests for the world Church. And so I became an ordinary diocesan priest and have never regretted it. I was ordained in Rome in 1933.

I am convinced that religion is part of our being. It is ingrained in us and that is why we need religious dialogue and personal prayer. We need religious dialogue because faith seeks community: 'Look, I am standing at the door knocking. If one of you hears me calling and opens the door, I will come in to share a meal at that person's side' (Revelation 3.20). And we need personal prayer because it is only through personal prayer that we become or are religious. I fully agree with Karl Rahner's memorable warning that if Christians did not become mystics there would soon be no Christians left. I would prefer to use the words 'personal prayer', however, as 'mystics' has so many different associations. If Christians no longer make a practice of personal prayer, there will indeed soon be no Christians left. Personal prayer is without doubt that form of prayer which brings us closest to God.

The personal search for God lies at the heart of religion. When we pray, we ask God for the wisdom to understand what is happening in the world and in our own hearts. We seek answers to those gnawing questions which keep surfacing: Where do I come from? Where am I going? What sense has my life?

And personal prayer is a dialogue. I am not addressing an empty space when I pray. My prayer has a focus. I am addressing him who loves me and whom we call God. I have often been asked, especially by young people, how one can begin to pray. In the course of what is now a very long life, I have learnt that the best way

122

to learn to pray is through practice. Simplicity is important. Prayer is very much an affair of the heart. What is important is to pray regularly and keep persevering. Begin by telling God in your own words what is moving you, what you are afraid of, but above all what you hope and long for. Start with the little things in your everyday life. Nothing, however trivial it may seem to you, is not important enough to be brought before God. And take heart, prayer works and is never in vain. All our prayers are answered, even if often in unexpected ways and at unexpected times. But prayer is also very demanding. It is a challenge. We are inclined to be indolent and have a deep aversion against anything which could upset us in any way or prove uncomfortable. And prayer is uncomfortable. There is also a risk involved. When we pray, we inevitably hear the voice of our conscience telling us what we should or should not do. The voice may say, 'You could make more of your life', or even suggest a complete change of mind and heart. These are challenges we must accept. Being or becoming a Christian is always a personal decision. Formerly, in a more or less closed Christian society, the personal decision seemed less important, but then the danger was greater that faith would be replaced by tradition. Today, in our pluralistic society, personal decisions and the consequences they have are far more necessary and important. It may be more difficult to be a Christian today, but when it succeeds, it is a far deeper commitment and involves one's whole being. A modern Christian's survival pack should contain all the important impulses of the Second Vatican Council; that is, the new image of the Church as the Pilgrim People of God, the importance of the laity in the Church and the commitment to ecumenical and inter-religious dialogue. The basis for all this, however, is personal faith and above all personal prayer, as through personal prayer we remain close to God and in his safe keeping.

In future, the example of individual Christians and an unassuming, simple Christian lifestyle will play a far more important role than Church organizations. We are still far too steeped in the tradition that it is imperative to make propaganda for the faith, and too convinced that religion needs the support of public opinion and of the state. The time has come to discard such ideas. Faith that comes from within must once again come to the fore, a faith that was partly eclipsed by an over-powerful Church structure. The Church is more than Church law and church organizations. More and more people nowadays reject the outward forms of Christianity but are at the same time looking for essential values. That is why the Church will have to change. One of the reasons why decentralization is so essential is in order to uncover the buried sources of personal faith, and by buried sources I mean religious experience. Being a Christian does not only mean keeping the commandments and obeying the rules, as I used to think as a child. Christianity has a message which can move, transform and profoundly fulfil people and bring them inner harmony and peace. We experience something that affects our whole being and gives us an insight into that infinite mystery which we call God, an insight that can never be obtained through reason alone. We must go back to showing people what the Christian faith has to offer and how it can make a difference to their lives.

At the same time, however, being a Christian can never be exclusively a personal matter: it must always be integrated into a community. We live in an age of individualism. Many people are only interested in their own well-being. Christians believe that it is not only a case of what is good for the individual that matters, however – it must also be good for the community. The great advantage of this view is that it is a third way between individualism and collectivism. Christianity is concerned with getting the individual and the community to join forces. We need both – order and freedom.

In the end it all depends on the question that has been one of the central questions of world history over the past 2,000 years, namely: 'Who is Jesus Christ?'

It was Christ himself who first put this question to his disciples and friends. 'Who do you say that the Son of Man is?' he asked them (Matthew 16.13), only to repeat the question more insistently almost immediately, 'But who do *you* say that I am?' Since Christ's death and resurrection this question has been directed at each one of us. If Jesus was only a man, albeit a man with extraordinary qualities, but nevertheless only a human being, then the question is insignificant. If, however, God took on a human form in Jesus Christ and speaks to us through him, then the question concerns each one of us, and no one can honestly ignore it.

What is that final mystery of our existence from which we come and towards which we are moving? Is all this questioning and searching left to us, as so many traditions and religions believe? Or has a Father in heaven given us the final answer to this question through Jesus Christ, as we are told in Hebrews 1.1: 'At many moments in the past and by many means, God spoke to our ancestors through the prophets; but in our time, the final days, he has spoken to us in the person of his Son, whom he appointed heir of all things . . .'

And so to this day we are all still faced with the same question: Is Jesus Christ a great religious leader but only a human being, or is a Father in heaven speaking to us through him in order to highlight those final major questions and offer us an answer? Christians are convinced of the latter.

9

The pull of God in a godless age: *The Tablet* Open Day Address 1999

Some time ago, a special report in *The Tablet* asked the disturbing question: 'Where have all the Catholics gone?' From the sobering data at hand, Gordon Heald, managing director of a well-known research institute in Britain, diagnosed that not only had Mass attendance on Sundays declined steadily in England and Wales over the past 30 years, but the figures for priestly ordinations, baptisms, first Communions, confirmations and particularly for church marriages had fallen steadily and dramatically year by year. While admitting that this made 'depressing reading', Heald cautioned that, as always, the figures must be seen in a broader context. The falling trend applied to all mainstream Christian Churches in the United Kingdom, and indeed to the entire European continent, he recalled.

Five weeks later Heald's special report prompted the Belgian Jesuit Jan Kerkhofs, a well-known priest and sociologist, to demonstrate that the declining figures in England and Wales were indeed reflected across Europe. Based on his book *Europe Without Priests* (1995), Kerkhofs particularly concerned himself with the diminishing number of Catholic priests in Europe. He gives the statistics for thirteen countries over the past twenty years – most of them in Western Europe. A very detailed analysis by Zulehner and Tomka this year shows similar figures or trends for Central and Eastern Europe with only few deviations. In the former communist East Germany, for example, 73 per cent of the population do not belong to any Church. The figures for the Czech Republic are similar. The negative statistics for Denmark and Sweden are common knowledge. From comprehensive data in the European Values Studies, Kerkhofs comes to the conclusion that there is a Europe-wide drift away from Christianity to a vague sort of agnosticism, leading to a postmodern, post-Christian secularization of Europe.

Samuel Huntingdon, whose controversial book *Clash of Civilizations* attracted worldwide attention when it first appeared in 1997, comes to a similar conclusion:

Declining proportions of Europeans profess religious beliefs observe religious practices, and participate in religious activities. This trend reflects not so much hostility to religion as indifference to it. Christian concepts, values and practices nonetheless pervade European civilization.

And that, according to Huntingdon, means that Europe, by the 'weakening of its central component, Christianity', is heading for a crisis.

The English religious sociologist David Martin, sometime chairman of the International Society for Religious Sociology, comes to a similar conclusion. In Europe, he says, liberation from any kind of religion, particularly from Christianity, has reached proportions that are unprecedented in modern times. 'Europe has become the only really secular continent in the world', he remarks. According to Martin, the influence of the Enlightenment, which originated in Europe, has now thoroughly penetrated every level in Europe, and Christianity has lost its meaning. The Vienna-born American religious sociologist Peter Berger not long ago concluded that Europe had become 'a church catastrophe'. A report on Europe in the *Herald Tribune* concluded somewhat nonchalantly that today Europe was 'the most godless quarter on earth'.

In 1992 the German weekly *Der Spiegel* looked into the question of whether religion had a future, or whether God had got lost, and commissioned an opinion poll to find 'what Germans believe'. The conclusion *Der Spiegel* came to was entitled 'Farewell to God'. 'Behold!' *Der Spiegel* said, 'the Germans have lost their belief in God and with it their Christian philosophy of life.' As it is no secret, however, that the editor of *Der Spiegel* inclines towards a negative view of Christianity, one could question his interpretation of the poll's results. It could have been influenced by his personal opinion.

Nonetheless, we must accept the fact that on the European continent at the present time the statistics and comparative figures point to a marked decline in religious practice, though some aspects of Church life cannot be measured statistically.

But there are other data which go in the opposite direction. Statistics for Africa and Asia show a marked increase in the number of Catholics on both continents. The Pope, as the ecumenical representative of the whole of Christianity, is held in high esteem worldwide, particularly outside Europe, and is given special attention in the media. *Time* magazine voted him 'Man of the Year' in 1994. In November 1995 the *Independent* said that the Pope was the only anchor in our chaotic world. And the innumerable tributes to Cardinal Hume on his death, not only from the United Kingdom, but from all over the world, were for an exemplary Christian of our time. I am told that Catholic and Anglican schools remain hugely popular in England. The same applies to other countries, above all to Austria.

Thus there is no lack of prominent voices proclaiming a worldwide religious renaissance, the first signs of which are already evident, they say. The French religious sociologist Gilles Kepel voices this opinion in his book *La Revanche de Dieu* (*God's Revenge*). American historians like Weigel and Huntingdon share his view. 'More broadly,' says Huntingdon, 'the religious resurgence throughout the world is a reaction against secularism, moral relativism, and self-indulgence, and a reaffirmation of the values of order, discipline, work, mutual help and human solidarity.'

The ecumenical Taizé movement for the young has had surprising success. A few years ago almost 100,000 young people from both Eastern and Western Europe flocked to Vienna for a Taizé meeting at Christmas. And in 1997 up to a million young people came to the World Youth Day in Paris to meet Pope John Paul II, albeit from a complexity of motives.

The Pull of God in a Godless Age

But this massive interest in religion is mostly outside the Christian Churches. The vast number of sects sends a strong signal that people generally find a religious vacuum intolerable for any length of time. For, as the study of religion and existentialist philosophy tells us, religion belongs to the essence of humanity: men and women seek a link to God or to a deity. It was Pascal who summed up the existential experience of the inquiring human mind with his famous words, 'The heart has its reasons which reason does not understand' – a sentence which has never lost its punch in the European history of ideas.

Notwithstanding widespread scepticism today regarding scientific advances and findings, there is a keen interest in atomic physics and astronomical occurrences. When, therefore, top scientists speak out on the question of God, this excites notice. In 1992 the Nobel Prize winner for physics (1984) and Director of the European Council for Nuclear Research (CERN: *Conseil Européen de Recherches Nucléaires*), Carl Rubbia, declared in an interview in the *Neue Zürcher Zeitung*:

When we list the number of galaxies or prove the existence of elementary particles, then this is probably not proof of the existence of God. But as a research scientist I am deeply impressed by the order and beauty that I find in the cosmos and within material phenomena. And as an observer of nature I cannot reject the thought that here a higher order of things exists in advance. I find the thought that all this is the result of coincidence or mere statistical diversity absolutely unacceptable. A higher

131

intelligence exists here over and above the existence of the universe itself.

Albert Einstein, the greatest physicist of this century, came to a similar conclusion. He himself did not adhere to any particular faith, but in his last essay on 'Science and Religion' he said:

My religion consists of a humble admiration of the unlimited spirit who reveals himself in the minutest details that we are able to perceive with our frail and feeble minds. That deeply emotional conviction of the presence of superior reasoning power is revealed in the comprehensible universe. That forms my idea of God.

The Second Vatican Council supplements such scientific assertions when it discusses the meaning of life. 'People look to their different religions for an answer to the unsolved riddles of human existence' says the Declaration on the Relation of the Church to Non-Christian Religions (*Nostra Aetate*, 1).

The problems that weigh heavily on people's hearts are the same today as in past ages. What is humanity? What is the meaning and purpose of life? Where does suffering originate, and what end does it serve? How can genuine happiness be found? What happens at death? What is judgement? What reward follows death? And finally, what is the ultimate mystery, beyond human explanation, which embraces our entire existence, from which we take our origin and towards which we tend?

We are all on a quest for the meaning and purpose of our lives. Neither a vague agnosticism nor a secularized environment can give answers to the unsolved mysteries of human life. So people look for the answers wherever they happen to be on offer, or wherever they happen to find them. For the search for the meaning and purpose of life is one of the key issues in philosophy, literature and psychiatry today. In Vienna, the late Viktor Frankl, a disciple of Freud's, based his therapy – logotherapy as he called it – on the quest for the meaning of our existence. This quest is not identical with the search for God but comes very close to it, he says. It is not a question of finding just any meaning for our existence, but of finding one for one's own life. Even erroneous expressions of religion in the diverse cultures are, in the last instance, the longing for a reliable answer to the ultimate questions of our existence, an answer to the insecurity of our lives.

It is the comparative study of religion that has shown us in all clarity that, as far as we know, there has never been a people or a tribe which had no religion. This fact alone shows that religion is closely linked to humanity, that it is a part of our being. Comparative religion thus proves that religious practice is an 'essential dowry' of the human soul.

If we open the book of history, we can see that in all places and at all times primitive peoples and the major religions of different civilizations have turned inquiringly and beseechingly to their God or gods. Wherever human beings have left us signs and monuments of their lives, we find proof they made sacrifices to their God and implored him for help. On all continents and at all times, human beings have knelt in supplication and praise, giving thanks and atoning to God, and have left us manifestations of their appeals and prayers so that aeons later we are able to look into their innermost beings.

The simple thanksgiving prayers of the Yamana on Tierra del Fuego, the supplications on Egyptian tombstones, their plaintive cries on small clay tablets immortalized in hieroglyphs, Chinese invocations to the heavens, Greek and Roman prayers of supplication for victory and success, the devotional chants of the Buddhist canon, the hymns of praise to the gods of the Vedic and Avestic pantheon in India and Persia – are a many-voiced, never-ending *Gloria* carved on rocks, written on clay or chiselled in stone. They are the moving *Miserere* and *De Profundis* of people who lived thousands of years ago and who implore superior powers to help and deliver them. As far back in the history of the world as it has been possible to trace human manifestations and civilizations, the traces and voices of supplicating, praying human beings accompany us.

And now by comparison, let us listen to the moving lament of someone who has given up the search for God, who refuses to pray any longer, and who raises his hands insistently against God. It is Friedrich Nietzsche, who set out to kill God; that is, to put man in God's place. Addressing himself, he says:

134

You will never pray again,
never adore again,
never again rest in endless trust.
You do not permit yourself to stop before any
    ultimate wisdom,
ultimate goodness, ultimate power,
while harnessing your thoughts.
You have no perpetual guardian and friend
for your seven solitudes.
You live without a view of mountains,
with snow on their peaks and fire in their hearts.
There is no avenger for you any more
nor any final improver.
There is no longer any reason in what happens,
no love in what will happen to you.
No resting place is open any longer to your heart,
where it only needs to find and no longer to seek.
You resist any ultimate peace . . .
Who will give you the strength for that?
No one has yet had this strength.
(Nietzsche, *Fröhliche Wissenschaft*, Aphorism 285)

This is the voice of the man who wanted to put himself
in God's place and perished in the process. What do these
contradictory views mean for us Christians at the
beginning of the new millennium? On the one hand, the
figures reflect a departure from the Church as a community of the faithful; but, on the other hand, we are
confronted with this longing for God.

What is the reason for the present decline of the Christian Churches? Is society to blame? Or is it because the

Christian Churches do not understand the signs of the times or do not want to understand them and are therefore failing to get their message across? Or is it the fault of the Christians themselves?

So, first, is society to blame?

In this century our society has become pluralistic and multicultural as never before. A far-reaching transformation is detectable far and wide. Science and technology have fundamentally changed our lives. Two world wars destroyed Europe. But the belief in scientific progress as a substitute for religion, which was strong at the beginning of the century, has begun to waver.

Already 35 years ago, with no knowledge of the statistics we have today on the diminishing interest in our Christian faith, the Second Vatican Council saw that

> the accelerated place of history is such that one can scarcely keep abreast of it. The destiny of the human race is viewed as a complete whole, no longer, as it were, in the particular histories of various peoples: now it merges into a complete whole. And so humankind substitutes a dynamic and more evolutionary concept of nature for a static one, and the result is an immense series of new problems calling for a new endeavour of analysis and synthesis. (*Gaudium et Spes*, 5)

A little later, the same *Gaudium et Spes* (9) noted that 'people are becoming conscious that the forces they have unleashed are in their own hands and that it is up to them to control them or be enslaved by them. Here lies the modern dilemma.' Thus the Council foresaw the dramatic social transformation that would take place by the beginning of the new millennium. And, at the end of the second millennium, the Council's prognosis has proved correct: in their desire for ever greater autonomy, individuals rely more and more on themselves and distrust any kind of institution. Authority is questioned. The outcome, on the one hand, is widespread insecurity and a loss of solidarity with one's fellow men and women. And on the other hand, egotism and arrogance have led to increased criticism of the state and society from which the Church, in its role as the Christian community of the faithful, has not been spared.

Public opinion has undergone a transformation. A dynamic and flexible media society has replaced the former stable order of firmly established institutions. A general change of values is gaining ground. Marriage and the family are particularly affected. Since the 1960s freedom and independence have become the slogans of the younger generation. But freedom without responsibility for oneself and for others is fragile.

Almost imperceptibly, the ambivalent power of the media is becoming the decisive factor in multicultural public opinion. Local events are frequently blown up to a global dimension these days, and single facts generalized. Everyone is convinced that they are perfectly informed and can therefore comment on and criticize the most distant of events. Everything is in a state of flux and anything seems possible. On the one hand we have a proliferation of knowledge and experience, a new willingness to help prompted by global access to information;

on the other hand, there is talk of 'the power of evil images', a climate of ruthlessness and violence which many link to the influence of the media. There seems to be a growing conviction that it is easier to solve conflicts by force than through dialogue. Where is Christianity's place in all this?

Second, is the decline the fault of the Churches?

With its breakneck speed, media society, which has eyes only for the human side of the Church, adds to the feeling of insecurity in Church practice. Thus, spread by one-sided media reporting, the negative image of the Church and of the Christian faith is blown up out of all proportion. Faced with such a scenario, Church leaders have become increasingly uneasy. Some try to withdraw from such a complex situation and turn their attention inwards. They busy themselves with self-criticism and attempts at structural reform. In post-conciliar discussions this tendency is further aggravated by the division between the 'conservatives' and the 'progressives'. A sort of 'Church navel-gazing' is taking place.

But the primary concern of the Christian Churches, of every Church, but particularly of the Catholic Church, in whose name I speak, cannot first and foremost be its public image. Its primary concern must always be to pass on the Gospel message with its partly adaptable and partly unalterable standpoint. And so I am faced with the question: how do I fulfil my task of conveying my message in the world as it is today? It is not an easy task and requires much more than it used to – honest co-operation between bishops, priests and laity. Here, too, it was the Second Vatican Council which repeatedly pointed to the necessity of such co-operation. As *Lumen Gentium* 33 says, 'Now, the laity are called in a special way to make the Church present and fruitful in those places and circumstances where only through them can it become the salt of the earth.'

And this, too, is the reason why Church leaders should not be afraid of too great a diversity. Over the years their fears in this respect have led to an excessive and defensive centralism and bureaucracy. Ever since the Second Vatican Council, it has become increasingly clear that the Catholic Church faces a problem of a particular kind in the future. The Catholic faithful in the parishes and dioceses lose heart when they receive no reassurance or comfort from the central Church leadership, when – with the exception of those documents and encyclical letters written by the Pope himself (I want to emphasize this) – warnings of error and heresy predominate in the countless documents that pour out of Rome. The Catholic faithful expect signs of encouragement and a mutual flow of information as a sign of unity and of diversity.

That is why the question of what kind of leadership the Catholic Church requires in order to preserve its unity in a rapidly changing world, and what forms of diversity are possible without seriously endangering that unity on the threshold of the third millennium, keeps cropping up nowadays. That Pope John Paul II was aware of this question is evident from his encyclical letter *Ut Unum Sint* (95), in which he recalls with emphasis the link between the college of bishops and the Pope. 'The bishop of Rome is a member of the college,' he says, 'and the bishops are his brothers in the ministry.'

The diversity of the Church must be given room – in reliance on the Holy Spirit – in every field and every issue of Church life. The community of the faithful is rooted in the families, the parishes, where people grow into the community and become Christians through baptism and the sacraments. It is these small, living communities which form the network of the Church with their knowledge of Christianity, their basic religious instruction for adults (catechism) and their faithful solidarity. In such turbulent times, this network needs information, communication, reinforcement and encouragement from the larger structures of the world Church which, according to the principle of subsidiarity, must be supportive and not dictatorial. Then the solidarity of the Church community will grow.

Third and finally, is the decline the fault of the Christians themselves?

God created living people and not structures. In the last instance it is always people we are dealing with. The best structures are no help if we human beings fail. That is what Jesus meant when he was teaching in Israel, and said after the Sermon on the Mount, as Matthew 5.13 tells us: 'You are the salt of the earth; but if salt has lost its taste, how shall its saltness be restored? It is no longer good for anything except to be thrown out . . . You are the light of the world. A city set on a hill cannot be hid . . . Let your light so shine before men, that they may see your good works and give glory to your Father who is in heaven.' And finally, 'Every one then who hears these words of mine and does them will be like a wise man who built his house upon a rock.'

This means that it is not enough to discuss the word of God and comment on it: we must above all carry it out and bear witness to it by the way we live. There is no spectacular answer, no secret recipe. The Churches, the faithful in the Churches, must be credible interpreters, witnesses of God's love for mankind. That is the secret of a Mother Teresa or a Fr Maximilian Kolbe, who changed the world around them. And so Christianity and its Churches do not have to invent anything new. They must simply go on proclaiming the same Gospel, not so much with words but through bearing loving witness by the way they live.

In order to highlight its endeavours to understand the world, the Second Vatican Council began its great pastoral constitution on the Church in the modern world with a renewed statement of Christian humanism: 'The joys and hopes, the grief and anguish of the people of our time, especially of those who are poor or afflicted, are the joys and hopes, the grief and anguish of the followers of Christ as well. Nothing that is genuinely human fails to find an echo in their hearts' (*Gaudium et Spes*, 1). With great momentum the Council produced the equipment for the Church's future course in its texts, with which one must be well acquainted. I can only mention a few key phrases here: the renewed image of the Church, the efforts to promote ecumenism, the co-operation of priests and laity, the significance of the major religions from the Christian point of view through inter-religious dialogue, and finally the emphasis on religious freedom.

To sum up: the Christian community in Europe, which from the Emperor Constantine's conversion in the fourth century onwards had the respect and support of public opinion, has today been thrown back on itself by a non-believing, indifferent, often even hostile environment, and as in its first beginnings is out on its own, left to its own resources which have evolved from both a divine and a human element. The traces of Constantine's Church would seem to be fading, and a second turning-point as fundamental as the Constantinian one confronts us. Faced with a cold wind of resistance, the ecumenically united Christian community is once again becoming the salt of the earth and the light on the mountains. For the call to be a light which shines from the mountain top, to be salt which does not lose its taste, holds good for the Christian way of life in all centuries.

Let us finally listen to the voice of a man for whom bearing witness was of the utmost importance:

Shine like a light in a world of darkness . . . One would not have to say this if our lives really did shine out. We would not need to tell if we let deeds speak.

There would be no heathens if we were true Christians, if we kept Christ's commandments. But we love money just as they (the heathens) do – in fact more than they do. We fear death as much as they do. How then are they to be convinced of our beliefs? By a miracle? There are no more miracles. By our behaviour? It is bad. By love? Not a trace of it anywhere. That is why one day we will have to account not only for our sins, but for the damage we have done.

The Pull of God in a Godless Age

The man who expressed his concern so forcibly was St John Chrysostom, Patriarch of Constantinople and a contemporary of St Augustine's in the fifth century.

What Chrysostom said when Christianity was in its beginnings holds true for us in our multicultural society today as we begin a new millennium. Words alone are not enough. Human beings and what they do are the decisive factor.

143